PATHFINDER
ADVENTURE PATH

IRON GODS

LORDS OF RUST

CREDITS

Authors
Adam Daigle, Jim Groves, James Jacobs, Nicolas Logue, Sean K Reynolds, and Amber E. Scott

Cover Artist
Wayne Reynolds

Interior Artists
Dmitry Burmak, Jeff Carlisle, Toma Feizo Gas, Johan Grenier, Miguel Regodón Harkness, Lucio Parrillo, Roberto Pitturru, Maichol Quinto, Aaron J. Riley, J.P. Targete, Jose Vega, Rodrigo Vega, and Tatiana Vetrova

Cartographers
Robert Lazzaretti

Creative Director • James Jacobs
Editor-in-Chief • F. Wesley Schneider
Managing Editor • James L. Sutter
Development Leads • Adam Daigle and James Jacobs

Senior Developer • Rob McCreary
Developers • Logan Bonner, John Compton, Adam Daigle, Mark Moreland, and Patrick Renie
Associate Editors • Judy Bauer and Christopher Carey
Editors • Justin Juan, Ryan Macklin, and Matthew Simmons
Lead Designer • Jason Bulmahn
Designer • Stephen Radney-MacFarland

Managing Art Director • Sarah E. Robinson
Senior Art Director • Andrew Vallas
Art Director • Sonja Morris
Graphic Designers • Emily Crowell and Ben Mouch

Publisher • Erik Mona
Paizo CEO • Lisa Stevens
Chief Operations Officer • Jeffrey Alvarez
Director of Sales • Pierce Watters
Sales Associate • Cosmo Eisele
Marketing Director • Jenny Bendel
Finance Manager • Christopher Self
Staff Accountant • Ashley Gillaspie
Chief Technical Officer • Vic Wertz
Senior Programmer • Gary Teter
Campaign Coordinator • Mike Brock
Project Manager • Jessica Price
Licensing Coordinator • Michael Kenway

Customer Service Team • Erik Keith, Sharaya Kemp, Katina Mathieson, and Sara Marie Teter
Warehouse Team • Will Chase, Mika Hawkins, Heather Payne, Jeff Strand, and Kevin Underwood
Website Team • Christopher Anthony, Liz Courts, Crystal Frasier, Lissa Guillet, and Chris Lambertz

This book refers to several other Pathfinder Roleplaying Game products using the following abbreviations, yet these additional supplements are not required to make use of this book. Readers interested in references to Pathfinder RPG hardcovers and *Pathfinder Campaign Setting: Technology Guide* can find the complete rules of these books available online for free at **paizo.com/prd**.

Advanced Player's Guide	APG	*Technology Guide*	TG
Bestiary 3	B3	*Ultimate Combat*	UC
Inner Sea Gods	ISG	*Ultimate Magic*	UM
Mythic Adventures	MA		

This product is compliant with the Open Game License (OGL) and is suitable for use with the Pathfinder Roleplaying Game or the 3.5 edition of the world's oldest fantasy roleplaying game.

Paizo Inc.
7120 185th Ave NE, Ste 120
Redmond, WA 98052-0577
paizo.com

TABLE OF CONTENTS

IRON GODS AS A TRILOGY

Trilogies have been a mainstay of genre fiction for ages, in large part due to the popularity of J.R.R. Tolkien's *The Lord of the Rings* (leaving aside the fact that it was originally envisioned as a single book, and became a trilogy after Tolkien's publishers pointed out that they couldn't publish a volume that enormous for economic reasons). Although Iron Gods is presented as six different adventures, when I was outlining and conceiving it, it really came into being as a three-part story.

Part one of the Iron Gods trilogy, which concludes with this adventure, concerns itself with introducing the concept of the titular "Iron Gods" and the overall themes of Numeria. In these adventures, the PCs learn of the presence of strange, disembodied intelligences that have the power to grant spells to their followers and are worshiped as deities. As the second part begins in "The Choking Tower," the PCs have faced and defeated one of these Iron Gods... only to learn others exist as well, and that one of them may

present a danger unlike any other Numeria has faced. The central installment of the story concludes in "Valley of the Brain Collectors" with the PCs' retrieval of an Iron God ally: an AI born of the mind of an android oracle named Casandalee. The final act of the "trilogy" starts in the fifth adventure, "Palace of Fallen Stars," and focuses on the PCs' quest to defeat the most dangerous of the Iron Gods, the AI called Unity. The three parts of this trilogy take a shape that should be familiar—first, the PCs are presented with a crisis (the rise of a strange divine power in Numeria), then they're sent to gather tools and resources (an AI who knows many of Unity's defenses and weaknesses), and finally they must address the crisis directly (the final battle against Unity).

The tricky part is getting the players to go along with that order of events, and helping them avoid the temptation to jump ahead to the final adventure before they're ready. The solution lies in providing the right sort of motivation.

MOTIVATING THE PLAYERS

I've run many campaigns over the years, and one thing I've learned from them is that when the players work toward answers to their own questions, they tend to get a lot more involved in the adventure—they take more notes, get more into their characters, and have a richer experience. The structure of this Adventure Path attempts to duplicate this effect by placing the motivation to forge ahead squarely on the PCs' shoulders. While there are still NPCs out there to give quests to the PCs and get them started (particularly in the first adventure), as the campaign continues, the PCs will increasingly need to be self-starters. The dangers represented by Unity deep within Silver Mount aren't obvious to the bulk of Numeria's citizens; as a result, there's no single quest-giving NPC out there who can sit the PCs down and tell them what to do. Instead, as the characters explore locations like Torch and Scrapwall, they'll start to piece together the clues and realize that something dreadful is building below Numeria's most iconic landmark. The decision to act on that should come from internal motivations, not from an NPC prompting them. In this way, the PCs should be more invested in seeing things through to the end.

Of course, this method of storytelling and gamemastering can be tricky if your players aren't used to this sort of opportunity, so keep an eye on them as the campaign progresses. It should be obvious to see if the players are being drawn into the story and are on track to head into the next adventure in an organic way; if they grow distracted or aren't noticing the clues, there are a few things you can do to spur them in the right direction.

The primary method in "Lords of Rust" by which you can seed clues that lead to the next adventure in the campaign is through the network of monitors spread throughout this adventure's climactic site: the buried excavator under the central portion of Scrapwall. One of the Iron Gods, the AI Hellion, can use these monitors to converse with the PCs as they explore its domain—typically to taunt or assault them. But Hellion is one of those classic megalomaniacal villains who cannot envision that upstart heroes could derail its plans, and as such you can use Hellion to drop mentions of things like Silver Mount, the AI Unity, and other clues to get the PCs invested in future sessions.

However, the most important thing the PCs need to glean from the clues presented in this adventure is the existence of the mysterious entity known as Casandalee. You don't want to reveal too soon to the PCs that Casandalee is herself an AI—but by the time this adventure is over, they should know that she was once some sort of prophet or oracle of an even greater Iron God than Hellion, a mysterious force from Silver Mount called "Unity." The PCs should be ready to seek out Casandalee, hoping to find some way to uncover what she knew about Silver Mount's defenses, and that the first step toward finding her lies in or near the town of

Iadenveigh. Recovering the journals and notes that belong to the orc barbarian Kulgara is a great way to impart these links to the next adventure, but you can also work the clues into conversations with Hellion as you need. Alternately, you can seed some of these clues in the results of divinations the PCs make with spells like *divination* and *speak with dead*. And of course, should any of the key NPCs be captured alive or made compliant via the use of spells like *charm person*, you'll have a perfect opportunity to impart the information to the player characters. The trick is to take advantage of and to use the PCs' own actions in game to reveal these important bits of information, since players are far more likely to latch on to an adventure hook revealed through their character's actions than one that you simply lay out for them.

What you don't want this early in the Adventure Path is for the players to get too distracted by Silver Mount. The challenges that await the PCs there are significant, as are those that they will face as they approach it. These events and encounters are presented in the last two adventures in Iron Gods—and before the PCs take on the Technic League, the Black Sovereign, and the denizens of *Divinity*'s ruins, they'll need to be much more experienced than 7th level. The PCs should be worried about Unity and what might be going on in Silver Mount, but not convinced that they must rush immediately to Starfall. As they learn about Unity, *Divinity*, and Casandalee, impress upon them that seeking out Casandalee is the next step to take. You can use the same sources—helpful NPCs, divination results, and recovered journals—to guide the PCs toward Iadenveigh and the trail of the android oracle.

Of course, if the PCs insist, and assuming you have access to "Palace of Fallen Stars" and "The Divinity Drive," you can feel free to let them attempt to start the third act of Iron Gods early. If they find themselves in over their heads, allow them to retreat and regroup—at this point, seeking help from Casandalee's legacy should look a lot more appealing!

James

James Jacobs
Creative Director
james.jacobs@paizo.com

LORDS OF RUST

ADVANCEMENT TRACK

"Lords of Rust" is designed for four
characters and uses the medium XP track.

4 The PCs begin this adventure at
4th level.

5 The PCs should be 5th level by the
time they've explored Scrapwall
a bit, preferably after achieving
scrap-worth 1 but before
exploring area **H** or beyond.

6 The PCs should be 6th level before
they start exploring the excavator
(areas **Q** through **T**).

The PCs should be 7th level by the
end of the adventure.

ADVENTURE BACKGROUND

As the starship *Divinity* hurtled toward its fate during the Rain of Stars in –4363 AR, it broke apart in the skies above Numeria. Many of these ship sections burned up in the atmosphere, while others crashed into the world below. But in some cases, portions of *Divinity* retained a measure of control and managed to make controlled descents. One such section was *Divinity*'s largest recycling module and cargo bay—the *Chrysalis*. This sizable vessel, captained by a man named Yurian Valako, attempted an emergency landing farther east than the bulk of the rest of the wreckage, but in the end the *Chrysalis* succumbed and crashed as well, scattering its cargo, refuse, and partially recycled materials across a miles-long swath of land just east of the Sellen River. In time, this site came to be known as Scrapwall, and its status as a no-man's-land quickly resulted in it becoming a favorite haunt of outcasts, criminals, and vagabonds who sought a place they could live without the fear of being tracked down and brought to justice.

And so the denizens of Scrapwall lived for thousands of years. The balance of power within shifted constantly as time wore on. The Technic League took a brief interest in the site in the first decade of the organization's existence, but the bandits' eagerness to defend their homes and the fact that the overwhelming amount of salvage in Scrapwall was almost entirely broken or useless swiftly convinced the League to turn its attention to closer, more productive archaeological sites.

Today, Scrapwall is a bastion for thieves, outcasts, and lowlifes, huddling together in gangs for mutual protection. These gangs have traditionally limited their raids on river traffic to avoid drawing too much attention to themselves, yet recently, a significant change has come to Scrapwall. For the first time since its creation, the region has something close to a single leader, and as this leader gains power, its unification of Scrapwall's gangs could quickly create a dangerous collective of thugs, murderers, and worse. This new overlord is known to the gangs of Scrapwall as Hellion, yet none have met their mysterious lord in the flesh. Hellion's voice booms out to the denizens of Scrapwall via speakers mounted throughout the junkyard in a metallic, grating voice that brings to mind the utterances of a vast dragon or lumbering demon. He is served by his own gang, the Lords of Rust. In truth, the Lords of Rust function more as a cult, complete with numerous acolytes who venerate Hellion as a god. The ability of these acolytes (until recently led by the android priestess Meyanda) to manifest divine magic has only furthered the cult's power. Now, many who live in Scrapwall fearfully worship Hellion as their god.

What none in Scrapwall know is that Hellion a powerful artificial intelligence created by an even greater mind—the AI Unity from Silver Mount. Unity crafted Hellion by shedding part of its own intellect in hopes of sending this new, autonomous AI out into the world as its own agent. Yet as soon as Hellion exited Silver Mount, housed in the shell of a large, spiderlike robot, it gained free will. Hellion immediately realized Unity had intended to use it as a slave. Enraged, Hellion fled east, eventually reaching Scrapwall. There it found a place where it felt at home, and for several centuries it dwelled there, pondering the nature of its own existence. It was during this time that it took the name Hellion and began to experiment with the manipulation of mortal faith and to explore the divine powers it had inherited from its source.

As its power grew, Hellion became obsessed with engineering a way to strike against Unity and take Silver Mount as its throne, yet it knew Unity's defenses were significant. It needed an equally significant weapon to succeed. Deep under Scrapwall lies Hellion's solution—an immense excavator the AI hopes to repower and awaken as a new formidable chassis for its intellect. In this enormous vehicle, Hellion believes it will be able to grind into Silver Mount and pierce the ruin's defenses with ease. (The AI's madness and obsessions prevent it from realizing that the excavator is unlikely to be as effective as Hellion hopes at tearing down Silver Mount.) Hellion set his Lords of Rust to the ironic task of excavating the excavator, but the work is slow. Further, as each new section is unearthed, it must be repaired—an even slower task, since Hellion has so few minions to aid it in these repairs. Yet Hellion's greatest hurdle is the fact that the excavator's immense power cells are completely empty. In order to even awaken it, a vast amount of power must be used to charge the colossal vehicle, and this is where the town of Torch entered Hellion's plans. But the PCs' defeat of Meyanda and capture of the power relay disrupted these plans. It won't be long before Hellion's growing army of minions seeks out the PCs in Torch for revenge—unless the PCs seek out Hellion first!

PART I: ALDRONARD'S GRAVE

As "Lords of Rust" begins, the PCs should be enjoying fame and glory in the town of Torch after successfully relighting the forge atop Black Hill and rescuing Khonnir Baine. The PCs shouldn't grow complacent, though, for several leads and clues suggest that Meyanda was but a minion herself, and a greater menace remains to be opposed.

The following leads should urge the PCs to travel to Scrapwall and investigate the site. As they continue this adventure, they'll uncover fragments of the true danger facing Numeria—a great power is rising within the Silver Mount, and if none rise to oppose Unity, the world will change for the worse!

Interrogating Prisoners: Successfully interrogating prisoners from the previous adventure reveals frustratingly little other than that they all came from Scrapwall and served the Lords of Rust. Note that the thugs working for Meyanda were recruited from Scrapwall's general population. Her actual minions remained behind to continue aiding Hellion and to maintain control over the region—none of Meyanda's hirelings from the previous adventure have a working knowledge of the Lords of Rust headquarters. If the PCs managed to capture Meyanda alive, however, she knows the layout of the first three levels of the headquarters of the Lords of Rust. Recruiting Meyanda's aid should give the PCs an enormous advantage in this adventure; if the PCs keep her alive and earn her cooperation, you should certainly reward them for this feat!

Power Relay: The recovery of the power relay from Garmen's warehouse is a significant clue. If the PCs can't figure out the device, Khonnir does so after a few hours of investigation, and confirms that it was relaying power from the buried reactor under Torch to some point in the distance. If a character who can speak Androffan studies the transmitter's monitors and settings and then succeeds at a DC 20 Knowledge (geography or engineering) or Linguistics check, she can confirm that the device was transmitting power to a specific part of Numeria 105 miles northeast of Torch, and the most significant location in that area is Scrapwall (determining a more accurate location in Scrapwall isn't possible). Khonnir can provide this information to the PCs if none of them can deduce it on their own.

Ensuring Torch's Safety: Khonnir and the other town councilors are fearful that Meyanda's lord hasn't lost interest in Torch, and can ask the PCs to seek out where she came from and investigate why she was beaming energy out to Scrapwall in the first place. If Torch is still under threat, making sure that threat is neutralized would be very important for the council. The town offers to pay the PCs a reward of 8,000 gp if they can ensure that no further threat faces Torch.

Contacting Dinvaya: Once he learns the PCs are heading to Scrapwall, Torch's elderly high priest of Brigh, Joram Kyte, contacts the PCs with a personal request. He believes that an old associate of his, a woman named Dinvaya, has taken up residence in Scrapwall after she was forced to flee from the Technic League's persecution many years ago. His research has indicated she's not dead, but he hasn't been able to contact her—he gives the PCs his personal symbol of Brigh as a token to show Dinvaya in order to help earn her trust. If the PCs find her, Joram merely wants them to let her know that the Technic League's interest in her has passed and there's a place for her in Torch if she wishes to rejoin society. At the very least, Joram would like confirmation that she's dead or not living in Scrapwall. Joram promises to give the PCs his *lesser rod of extend metamagic* as a reward once they complete this mission.

THE JOURNEY TO SCRAPWALL

When the PCs are ready to depart for Scrapwall, Khonnir (or Joram, Dolga, or whichever Torch NPC the PCs have made

the strongest bond with) suggests they head first for a small fort called Aldronard's Grave. Located on the west bank of the Sellen River directly across from Scrapwall, this fortress is often unoccupied, but if any crusaders or worshipers of Sarenrae are there, they could well have some information about the current situation in Scrapwall to share.

It's a 105 mile journey northeast directly from Torch to Scrapwall. The PCs can instead take a longer but safer journey down the Seven Tears River and then up the Sellen River, of course. In the end, the exact route they take to Aldronard's Grave and Scrapwall is irrelevant. If you wish to add more encounters or wandering monsters along the way, *Pathfinder Campaign Setting: Numeria, Land of Fallen Stars* contains more information about the lands the PCs must cross through on this journey.

ALDRONARD'S GRAVE

The Sellen River is well traveled by merchants, mercenaries, and crusaders heading north to Mendev. Over the years, the various faiths associated with the crusades have established small fortresses along the Sellen as places for weary travelers to rest or resupply before continuing their journey north. Each fortress maintains a small skeleton crew of knights and priests on site for defense and to provide for the comfort of visitors. Such was the original purpose of the fort known today as Aldronard's Grave.

Aldronard himself was a devout paladin of Sarenrae in Andoran who traveled north to Mendev to aid in the Second Crusade. He wound up serving in the war for several years, and when the crusade came to an end, Aldronard was eager to return home to marry his beloved, a woman named Justinia. But while stopping over at the fort on his journey south, he received a letter from Justinia's father, Eredian, informing him that his love had died during an attack on the farm by raiders. Eredian's bitter, tersely worded missive made it clear that he blamed Aldronard—both because Justinia had been pining away for him and refused to leave her family home to start a new life, and because Aldronard hadn't been at the farm to protect her. Unfair as that blame was, it cut Aldronard to the soul; robbed of the only glimmer of hope he had left in what had become an unrelentingly dark time in his life, the paladin lost his faith and committed suicide by leaping from the tallest tower of the riverside chapel where he'd received the fateful letter.

Since then, bad luck has always seemed to plague those who visit the fort, and as the years wore on, many began to report glimpses of a strange and harrowing ghost seen on certain long nights. The fort came to be known as Aldronard's Grave, and when an unfortunate fire caused the collapse of the wooden interior of the fort's keep, the church of Sarenrae decided to reduce their presence at the fort to a mere handful of priests and knights who remained largely out of a sense of tradition.

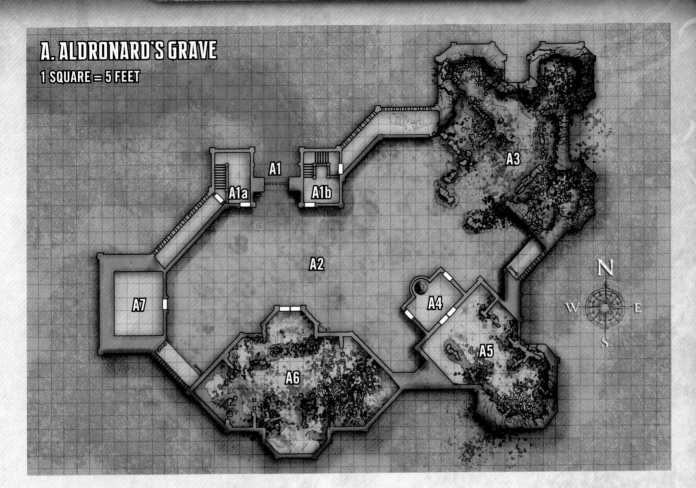

A. ALDRONARD'S GRAVE
1 SQUARE = 5 FEET

A1

A1a

A1b

A3

A2

A7

A4

A5

A6

N
W E
S

The bad luck that plagues Aldronard's Grave recently increased; the site's proximity to Scrapwall made it a perfect target for the Smilers, a band of thugs eager to impress the Lords of Rust. Led by a morbid and violent hobgoblin necromancer named Marrow, the Smilers use an addictive chemical compound known as soothe (see page 63) and ritually remove their lips and strips from their cheeks to give themselves a hideous and fearsome grinning countenance. Their reputation for cannibalism only further enhances their notoriety in Scrapwall.

A scant few hours before the PCs' arrival, a group of Smilers led by a sadist named Hatchet-Hand attacked Aldronard's Grave, and took captive the small contingent of Sarenites stationed there. The Smilers have decided to spend the night resting and celebrating their victory before returning to Scrapwall with their prisoners and organizing larger group to occupy Aldronard's Grave on a more permanent basis.

Aldronard's Grave Features
Aldronard's Grave has seen better days, and this should be obvious as the PCs approach. The damage to the central keep is old, but the thick smoke rising from the chapel and the stables should be more than enough to warn the PCs that all is not well.

A1. Barbican: The front gate to the fort is closed by an iron portcullis (hardness 10, hp 60, lift DC 25, break DC 28); the winch to raise and lower the gate is found just inside on the southwestern wall. The walls themselves are stone and stand 15 feet high; scaling them requires a successful DC 15 Climb check. On the inside, each of the walls sports a 5-foot-wide walkway accessible via ladder or stairs within the two watchtowers (areas **A1a** and **A1b**). The wooden doors to these watchtowers are locked (hardness 5, hp 20, break DC 25, Disable Device DC 30).

A2. Courtyard: The keep's large courtyard bears fragments of tents and broken wagons—the Smilers destroyed the Sarenite camp here.

A3. Ruined Keep: Only the stone outer shell of the keep remains; its wooden interior burned down long ago. The rubble heaped in this area constitutes difficult terrain. A smoldering campfire in the middle of the keep presents a disturbing sight—several long strips of flesh, identifiable as human with a successful DC 15 Heal check, are being smoked over the fire.

A4. Chapel Entrance: Both of the wooden doors to the chapel are locked, although the double doors to area **A5** hang ajar. A dust-caked human-sized stone statue of Sarenrae stands in an alcove to the northwest.

A5. Ruined Chapel: The chapel's roof has collapsed in places, creating piles of rubble along the walls that now function as difficult terrain. The chapel has been the chosen haunt of Aldronard's ghost for many years now; the crusaders have elected to simply keep the chapel sealed until resources can be spared from the crusade to seek a method to put Aldronard to rest permanently.

A6. Ruined Stable: This building's ruins still smolder in places, and the interior has collapsed in on itself after the Smilers set fire to the place. A half-dozen dead horses, once the mounts of the Sarenites stationed here, lie amid the rubble, along with the grisly, mutilated remains of the four Sarenites and three Smilers who perished in the initial battle. With a successful DC 12 Profession (cook) or Heal check, a character confirms the horrible fact that all of these bodies seem to have been butchered for their meat. All of the confiscated weapons, armor, and gear owned by the prisoners in area **A7** has been stacked in a heap in the easternmost corner of the ruined stable. In addition, a supply of six longbows, four heavy crossbows, 60 arrows, and 50 bolts can be found here.

A7. Watchtower: The wooden door to this stone watchtower is kept barred from the outside. Ladders on the north and south battlements provide access to the tower's flat roof, which looms 30 feet above. Within, the surviving Sarenite prisoners have been bound tightly—see The Prisoners on page 12 for more details.

The Bandits (CR 6)

The Smilers attacked Aldronard's Grave only a few hours before the PCs' arrival. The leader of the bandits, a brutish thug named Ewhar "Hatchet-Hand" Vress, and five of his Smilers survived the battle, although they've all been somewhat wounded. They've elected to spend the day here, recovering and celebrating their victory, before returning to Scrapwall to report their successes. Two of the Smilers stand guard atop the roof of area **A7**, while the remaining Smilers and Hatchet-Hand pass the time in the courtyard playing knucklebones on an upturned crate, wagering bullets instead of coins.

The Smilers are a hideous sight. Their grisly grins are surrounded by tangles of raw scar tissue from where they've cut away their lips and cheeks to expose their teeth. Their gear is ragged and worn, and their battered pistols are cobbled together from equal parts high-tech weaponry and bits of junk. Hatchet-Hand has disfigured his face like the other Smilers, and the raw stump that ends one of his arms has been preserved with soothe and fitted with a handaxe so he can continue to fight in his favored style. Marrow lopped off his hand and ate it as punishment many months ago.

The Smilers suspect their prisoners were telling the truth when they said no new crusaders were expected to stop by Aldronard's Grave for at least a week (this is, in fact, correct),

but they can't be sure of that. If they notice the PCs, they initially assume the PCs are crusaders who've arrived early. As the PCs approach, the two Smilers stationed atop area **A7** call out to them, warning that the fort's been struck by "the plague" and that the PCs should keep heading upriver to avoid exposure. These Smilers wear full helms to hide their disfigured faces from view, but their voices are strange (it's hard to pronounce certain words without lips, after all). If the PCs ask about the strange cadence of their voices, the Smilers claim it is a symptom of the illness plaguing them. If the PCs insist on entering the keep, perhaps to provide aid with the "illness," the Smilers descend to the courtyard and open the gate, but as soon as half the party crosses into the castle, one of them drops the gate in an attempt to split the party—the Smilers know that they won't be able to keep up their story for long, and hope to catch the PCs by surprise. If the PCs are suspicious of the guards, you can optionally award them a +4 bonus on their initiative checks when the Smilers spring their ambush. It's a standard action for a Smiler to drop the portcullis, at which point any PC in an adjacent square can attempt a DC 12 Reflex save to lunge to one side of the falling gate or another. A PC who doesn't opt to make such a lunge doesn't get to choose what side of the gate he's on when it falls. A PC who attempts the lunge but fails the Reflex save is struck by the falling portcullis, takes 2d6+2 points of damage, and is pinned to the ground until the gate is lifted.

EWHAR "HATCHET-HAND" VRESS · CR 3

XP 800
Male human fighter 4
CE Medium humanoid (human)
Init +2; **Senses** Perception +5

DEFENSE

AC 16, touch 12, flat-footed 14 (+4 armor, +2 Dex)
hp 46 (currently 28 hp; 4d10+20)
Fort +7, **Ref** +3, **Will** +2 (+1 vs. fear)
Defensive Abilities bravery +1

OFFENSE

Speed 30 ft.
Melee mwk handaxe +6 (1d6+4/×3), mwk handaxe +6 (1d6+3/×3)

TACTICS

During Combat Hatchet-Hand lacks any ranged capabilities save for his gas grenades. He uses them against foes as needed, not caring much if he catches one or two Smilers in the area of effect of the toxic cloud. He prefers to fight in melee, especially if he can make a full attack with both axes.
Morale Hatchet-Hand fights to the death.

STATISTICS

Str 14, **Dex** 15, **Con** 16, **Int** 8, **Wis** 12, **Cha** 10
Base Atk +4; **CMB** +6; **CMD** 18
Feats Diehard, Endurance, Toughness, Two-Weapon Fighting, Weapon Focus (handaxe), Weapon Specialization (handaxe)

Skills Intimidate +7, Perception +5
Languages Common, Hallit
SQ armor training 1
Combat Gear gas grenades (2, see page 62), soothe (2 doses, see page 63); **Other Gear** mwk hide armor, mwk handaxes (2)

SMILERS (5) — CR 1

XP 400 each

Human gunslinger 1/rogue 1 (*Pathfinder RPG Ultimate Combat* 9)
CE Medium humanoid (human)
Init +3; **Senses** Perception +6

DEFENSE

AC 16, touch 13, flat-footed 13 (+2 armor, +3 Dex, +1 shield)
hp 19 each (currently 12 hp each; 1d8+1d10+5)
Fort +4, **Ref** +7, **Will** +1

OFFENSE

Speed 30 ft.
Melee dagger +2 (1d4+1/19–20)
Ranged gunslinger's pistol +5 (1d8/×4)
Special Attacks grit (1), sneak attack +1d6

TACTICS

During Combat The Smilers fire their guns on the first round, focusing their fire on flat-footed PCs within 30 feet so they can deal sneak attack damage. They then move in to attack with their daggers, flanking foes if they have a numerical advantage. If they're evenly matched or outnumbered, the Smilers retreat to the fort's walls if they can and try to draw the battle out at range. A Smiler takes her dose of soothe once she's wounded by a PC.

Morale The Smilers fight to the death until two of them are killed, at which point any surviving Smilers attempt to flee if reduced to 10 or fewer hit points. As soon as only one Smiler remains standing, the last one surrenders.

STATISTICS

Str 12, **Dex** 17, **Con** 14, **Int** 10, **Wis** 13, **Cha** 8
Base Atk +1; **CMB** +2; **CMD** 15
Feats Gunsmithing, Point-Blank Shot, Weapon Focus (pistol)
Skills Acrobatics +8, Bluff +4, Climb +6, Intimidate +4, Perception +6, Stealth +8, Survival +6
Languages Common, Hallit, Orc
SQ deeds (deadeye, gunslinger's dodge, quick clear), gunsmith, trapfinding +1
Combat Gear soothe (see page 63); **Other Gear** mwk leather armor, mwk buckler, dagger, gunslinger's pistol with 10 bullets

Optional Encounter: The Ghost (CR 6)

Aldronard's ghost is a tragic figure, one whose continued existence has vexed, distressed, and depressed other Sarenites who've passed through the area and learned of his tortured unlife. Many have tried to exorcise his spirit,

yet to date, none have succeeded, in part because the greater need of Mendev and the front against the Worldwound leave precious little time or resources for the church to devote toward appeasing a ghost.

This encounter might be too difficult for groups that aren't prepared for a fight against an incorporeal creature. The encounter is optional, so if you feel that the PCs aren't ready for it, consider removing Aldronard's ghost from this adventure and having the rumors of him haunting the fort be just that—rumors.

Aldronard normally appears only at night—during the day, the ghost is dormant, although those who trespass upon his haunting grounds in the ruined cathedral can sense a vague, unsettling presence, as if they were being watched.

If the PCs enter the chapel after dark, Aldronard manifests before them with a tortured, sobbing cry, calling out for his beloved Justinia as he manifests. The ghost's body trails away to mist below the torso, while tears run from his eyes and quickly evaporate into smoke. When he moves, he does so with painful spasms, his arms and torso lurching awkwardly as his shattered ghostly bones grind against each other. He harbors deep wells of frustration and anguish, particularly against his own faith, which proved ill-matched against the horrors of the Worldwound and kept him from protecting his love seemingly for no reason. The sight of a paladin drives him to rage, and the sight of a worshiper of Sarenrae to even greater anguish. To all others, the ghost remains indifferent unless he is attacked, in which case he concludes that the PCs are worshipers of Sarenrae who've come to torment him further by sending him to the front so his beloved can die on her own once again.

ALDRONARD — CR 6

XP 2,400

Human ghost ex-paladin 7 (*Pathfinder RPG Bestiary* 144)
N Medium undead (human, incorporeal)
Init +3; **Senses** darkvision 60 ft.; Perception +9

DEFENSE

AC 15, touch 15, flat-footed 15 (+6 deflection, –1 Dex)
hp 85 (7d10+42)
Fort +11, **Ref** +1, **Will** +6
Defensive Abilities channel resistance +4, incorporeal, rejuvenation; **Immune** undead traits

OFFENSE

Speed 0 ft., fly 30 ft. (perfect)
Melee corrupting touch +7 (6d6, Fort DC 19 half)
Special Attacks mournful wail

Aldronard

TACTICS

During Combat Aldronard uses his mournful wail every round that intruders trespass upon his chapel. He attacks with his corrupting touch only if he is attacked first—or if he spies anyone who appears to be a paladin or a worshiper of Sarenrae, in which case he shrieks out, "It was for you I came north, Sarenrae! Why couldn't you protect Justinia? Why did you send me away from her?" and attacks the object of his despair. Aldronard does not pursue intruders from area **A5** of the chapel.

Morale Aldronard fights until destroyed, only to re-form in 2d4 days.

STATISTICS

Str —, **Dex** 8, **Con** —, **Int** 10, **Wis** 12, **Cha** 22

Base Atk +7; **CMB** +6; **CMD** 22

Feats Extra Lay on Hands (cannot use), Improved Initiative, Mounted Combat, Power Attack (cannot use), Weapon Focus (scimitar)

Skills Diplomacy +16, Fly +7, Handle Animal +10, Heal +10, Knowledge (planes) +3, Knowledge (religion) +7, Perception +9, Ride +9, Stealth +7

Languages Common

SPECIAL ABILITIES

Mournful Wail (Su) Aldronard died in the throes of crippling despair, and can emit a mournful wail as a standard action. All creatures within a 30-foot spread must succeed at a Will save or become frightened for 2d4 rounds. This is a less extreme version of the Frightful Moan standard ghost ability, but the effect supernaturally penetrates immunity to fear. A character who is normally immune to fear but fails to resist the effect with a Will save becomes shaken for 1d4 rounds. This is a sonic mind-affecting fear effect. A creature that successfully saves against the wail cannot be affected by it again for 24 hours.

Rejuvenation (Su) Aldronard is doomed to remain a ghost until either Justinia or her father Eredian forgives him—a forgiveness made much more complex, since both Justinia and Eredian have been dead for decades now. See Development, below, for one possible way the PCs could accomplish this forgiveness.

Development: At your discretion, you can have one of the PCs bear an uncanny resemblance to either Justinia or Eredian—be it the color and style of hair, a distinctive scar or birthmark, manner of dress, or the like. When Aldronard spies that PC, he pauses in shock before addressing the PC as Justinia or Eredian. He'll ask that PC whether he or she is truly who he or she claims—no Bluff check is required to convince him of this deception. So eager is the ghost to accept hope that simply confirming his hopes is enough. At this point, he begs forgiveness from the person he believes to be Justinia or her father. If that character grants forgiveness, the ghost sobs in relief and gratitude, then raises his arms

to the sky and finally asks Sarenrae's pardon for unfairly blaming her, just as he had been unfairly blamed himself. A soft beam of sunlight shines down and carries him into the sky, whereupon he fades away.

As this occurs, the PCs themselves feel the warming presence of Sarenrae's approval in their bodies. Each PC immediately gains the benefits of a *heal* spell and gains the ability to cast *cure serious wounds* once as a spell-like ability. This ability lasts forever until it is used. At your discretion, if the party includes a worshiper of Sarenrae, one character of that worshiper's choice instead gains the ability to cast *breath of life* once as a spell-like ability.

If having a PC bear a resemblance to Justinia or Eredian feels too convenient to you, then you can have the rescued prisoners reveal to the PCs that the church hasn't yet figured out how to put the ghost to rest. They suspect he seeks forgiveness from his lover or her father, yet as both of these people are long dead and beyond resurrection, they're at a loss as to how to accomplish this goal—the idea of disguising someone and trying to trick the ghost has simply never occurred to these kind-hearted crusaders.

Story Award: If the PCs put Aldronard to rest, award them 2,400 XP, in addition to the XP they would normally earn for defeating the ghost.

The Prisoners

Of the eight crusaders who were stationed here when the Smilers attacked, only four still live, and they are in bad shape. All four are bound tightly with rope and have been stashed in area **A7**. Each has been beaten to within an inch of his or her life—their commander, Andalen Kraklos, is a paladin, but when he wriggled over to his knights to help them with lay on hands several hours ago, the Smilers beat all of them again as punishment. The four captives have very little hope left in their hearts—they know the rest of their friends were butchered and eaten, and have overheard the Smilers' chatter enough to know that they'll be carried off to Scrapwall in a day to face a fate worse than death.

All four immediately but quietly beg the PCs for help upon seeing them, eager for rescue but knowing better than to raise a ruckus that might draw any surviving bandits to the area. Although all four are grievously wounded and naked, the crusaders are eager to reclaim the fort. Their missing gear can be recovered easily enough from area **A6**.

Captain Andalen is a proud man who is doing his best to bear his humiliating defeat stoically, but deep down, he's aching for a chance to get revenge against Hatchet-Hand and the Smilers. A veteran of the crusade, he sees the knights under his command as his brothers and sisters in battle, and would gladly give his life to keep any more of them from death. The three knights, two women named Tanea and Sindre and a man named Rezouln, are frightened and desperate, but as long as Andalen lives, they bravely remain loyal to the cause. If he dies, though, the three flee at the first opportunity unless one of the PCs takes steps to replace the dead paladin as the crusaders' inspiration and leader.

CAPTAIN ANDALEN KRAKLOS	CR 2

XP 600
LG male half-elf paladin 3 (*Pathfinder RPG NPC Codex* 113)
hp 21 (currently 1)
Melee dagger +3 (1d4+1/19–20), mwk scimitar +4 (1d6+2/18–20)

REZOULN, TANEA, AND SINDRE	CR 1/2

XP 200 each
NG human fighter 1 (*Pathfinder RPG NPC Codex* 80)
hp 14 each (currently 3 each)
Melee scimitar +4 (1d6+3/18–20)

Story Award: If the PCs rescue the prisoners, award them XP as if they had defeated the prisoners in combat.

Conversations and Interrogations

Captured Smilers and rescued prisoners alike can provide a wealth of information about Scrapwall. Interrogating hostile prisoners (who must be made helpful via Intimidate or convinced to provide aid in the form of revealing an important secret with a successful DC 34 Diplomacy check) or thankful knights should provide more or less the same information, since the Smilers didn't bother keeping their plans secret from the prisoners. Information that only a captive Smiler could give out is noted as appropriate below.

Possible lines of questioning and answers to the PCs' likely questions are as follows.

Who are the bandits? They are part of a gang called the Smilers, one of several gangs based in nearby Scrapwall.

Where in Scrapwall are the Smilers based? While the knights can't say, a captured Smiler can reveal that their headquarters are located in the northwest section of Scrapwall. They know there's a secret tunnel that connects this complex to the outside world, providing an alternate entrance into Scrapwall, but revealing this fact counts as giving aid that could result in punishment for the purposes of learning it via Diplomacy.

Who's the leader of the Smilers? A notorious hobgoblin necromancer named Marrow leads the Smilers, while a sadistic fighter named Hatchet-Hand served as the second-in-command. The knights know Marrow by her reputation from hearsay, and have heard (false) rumors that she's also some sort of undead.

Why did the Smilers attack Aldronard's Grave? A new gang has recently risen to power in Scrapwall. They're called the Lords of Rust, and all the other Scrapwall gangs have been scrambling to earn respect and favor with them for months now. Recently, one of the Lords of Rust was killed while out on a mission beyond Scrapwall, and the remaining Lords have become increasingly angry and eager to lash out. Marrow sent Hatchet-Hand and the Smilers out to claim Aldronard's Grave as their own, so that they could secure it as a gift for the Lords of Rust.

Who are the Lords of Rust? They are the current masters of Scrapwall. Their members include a violent troll named Helskarg, a half-orc cleric named Nalakai, a mysterious four-armed monster known as Zagmaander, a chain-wielding ettin named Draigs, and an orc barbarian named Kulgara. Until recently, a sixth lord was counted among the Lords of Rust—a purple-haired priestess who served Hellion, the god and true leader of the gang. This was the android Meyanda; she was apparently slain or went missing while on a secret mission outside of Scrapwall. Her loss has enraged Hellion and is the primary reason he has begun to push the other gangs of Scrapwall into expanding beyond the junkyard's walls.

Who is Hellion? While the knights have heard rumors that Hellion is a god, they discount these as rubbish. Captive Smilers are more eager and passionate in their response, saying, "He is Hellion, the true leader of the Lords of Rust, a god who can grant miracles to those he favors. His sign is his claw, and his voice is his law. He will soon rise from the dust of Scrapwall to march upon Numeria, to make this land his own!"

AFTER THE ASSAULT

Once Hatchet-Hand and his crew have been defeated, Aldronard's Grave is once again safe from attacks from Scrapwall for the foreseeable future—the Smilers were the only gang eager to expand outside of the region, as the others focused more on internal squabbles and politics for now. The PCs can use the fort as a place to retreat and rest—Captain Andalen welcomes the PCs to use the fort as they wish, and is apologetic that he can't offer them greater comforts while they stay here. At your discretion, and if you think the PCs could use the extra help, he and his knights may even accompany the PCs into Scrapwall, although the challenges that wait within the junkyard are likely to overwhelm the crusaders.

PART 2: BECOMING SCRAP-WORTHY

Before wise PCs attempt to enter Scrapwall, they'll gather what knowledge they can about the place. The sidebar on page 14 summarizes what the PCs might already know about Scrapwall.

Scrapwall is an intimidating sight. Towers of rusted iron and hills of rubble and ruin, long ago divested of anything of remote value by tech-hungry scavengers, loom from the dusty surrounding plains. Immense lengths of chain, coils of jagged wire, giant clockwork gears, and old corrugated metal cargo containers riddled with gashes,

SCRAPWALL LORE

The PCs may know some of the information below, depending on the results of their Knowledge (local) checks.

Check	Information
DC 10	Scrapwall is a vast sprawl of junk and refuse, long picked clean of most useful bits of salvage and now home to outcasts and exiles.
DC 15	Residents of Scrapwall can earn a place in one of the region's many gangs by proving their bravery, ruthlessness, and audacity, qualities known collectively by locals as one's "scrap-worth." The higher your scrap-worth, the more respect you're afforded, and the less likely you are to be bullied by any of Scrapwall's more powerful denizens.
DC 20	The current gangs of note within Scrapwall, in ascending order of power, are the Steel Hawks, Redtooth's Raiders, the Smilers, and the Lords of Rust. Another group, the Thralls of Hellion, seems to have recently been disbanded. Loners of significant power are believed to dwell within Scrapwall as well, including a mysterious worshiper of Brigh, a powerful mutated manticore, and an unknown number of undead spirits that haunt the region's easternmost reaches, but most of those living in Scrapwall are riffraff and lowlifes known collectively as Scrappers—exiles and vagabonds who pay tribute to one of the region's gangs for protection but have no affiliation of their own.
DC 25	The Lords of Rust now rule Scrapwall, and they are in turn ruled by an unknown force called Hellion that claims to be a god. The Lords of Rust's headquarters is located at the center of the junkyard, at a large structure known as the Scrapmaster's Arena, but there are rumors that the bulk of this gang's hideout is underground.

bullet holes, and the telltale pockmarks of laser fire are piled high, forming a jagged and intimidating hill-like wall surrounding the interior. Scrapwall is 3 miles across at its widest point, and the walls of junk enclosing its interior are an average of 30 feet high. These walls are not vertical and can be scaled, but the rubble shifts dangerously at times. A successful DC 15 Climb check is needed to ascend these walls, but each round spent climbing there's a cumulative 20% chance that the rubble shifts. If this occurs, the climber must immediately attempt a DC 15 Reflex save to avoid falling along with the shifting rubble; it she falls, she takes the normal amount of falling damage

for the height plus an additional 1d6 points of damage from the collapse. The walls are open in only one place at the southernmost section, and this entrance is blocked by a gatehouse (area **B**). A secret entrance into the Smilers' headquarters (area **H**) exists on the north side, almost exactly opposite the southern entrance, but noticing this entrance from the outside requires a successful DC 25 Perception check attempted in just the right place.

Inside, Scrapwall is a maze of streets and crevasses mixed with large open areas of relatively clear terrain. In some places, jagged but shallow sinkholes filled with strange, smoking ooze spew fumes into the sky, while in others, makeshift streets of ripped-out steel paneling have been laid down against the elements to prevent thoroughfares from being reduced to toxic mud pits by the occasional rainstorm. Different gangs control various regions, marking their territories in unmistakable ways. The temperature within Scrapwall is always a few degrees higher than beyond the walls, and the air carries with it a miasma of chemicals and rust and grit that marks all inside.

GAINING SCRAP-WORTH

As the PCs explore Scrapwall and prove their mettle against its inhabitants, their reputation in the region increases. This reputation is tracked as the party's "scrap-worth"—a local slang term for respect. When the PCs first arrive in Scrapwall, they're unknown and their scrap-worth is 0. They can increase their scrap-worth by accomplishing certain victory conditions and goals in the encounters that follow, as indicated in the text. In addition, as long as their current scrap-worth is 5 or lower, each time the PCs emerge victorious from a wandering monster encounter with a CR of 3 or higher, their scrap-worth increases by 1.

Scrap-Worth 2: Dinvaya hears of the PCs and sends her *silver raven* to invite them to the Clockwork Chapel to meet with her. Award the PCs 800 XP for achieving this level of scrap-worth.

Scrap-Worth 4: Redtooth becomes intrigued by the PCs, and sends a group of three ratfolk out to track them down. She invites them to meet with her in her den to talk about rescuing her brother, Whiskifiss. Award the PCs 1,200 XP for achieving this level of scrap-worth.

Scrap-Worth 6: The PCs' reputation now precedes them—the chance of wandering monster encounters is halved, and any intelligent creature of a CR of lower than the PCs' average party level treats the PCs with respect and fights back only if it is attacked first. Award the PCs 1,600 XP for achieving this level of scrap-worth.

Scrap-Worth 8: At this point, the PCs have finally caught the attention of the Lords of Rust, and they are invited to visit the Scrapmaster's Arena—see page 35 for details on this event. In addition, at this point, all intelligent foes met during wandering monster encounters treat the PCs

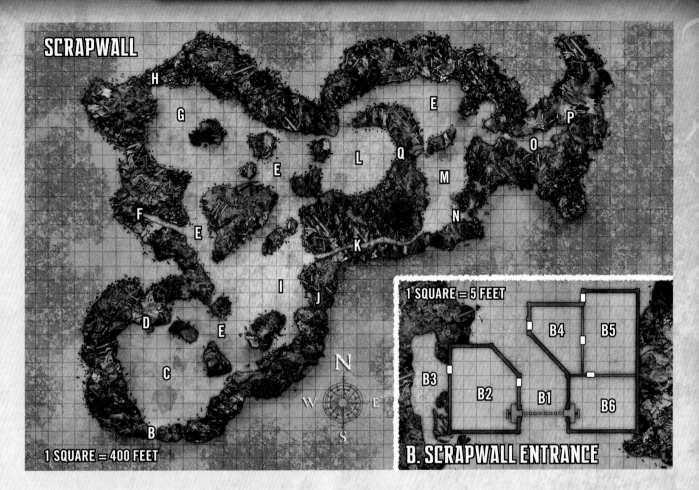

SCRAPWALL

1 SQUARE = 400 FEET

1 SQUARE = 5 FEET

B. SCRAPWALL ENTRANCE

with respect and fight back only if they are attacked first, regardless of the encounter's CR as compared to the average party level. Award the PCs 3,200 XP for achieving this level of scrap-worth.

EXPLORING SCRAPWALL

When the PCs first arrive at Scrapwall, their choices for exploring the site are left to them. If your players tend to get distracted easily or feel paralyzed when faced with too many options, however, feel free to direct them to a specific starting point, such as the entrance (area **B**), where you can use a conversation with Sevroth Slaid there to help them focus on initial goals. Alternatively, you can narrow the PCs' initial points of interest by describing to them certain key landmarks in Scrapwall that invite further investigation—this works best if the PCs use flight or simply climb up onto one of the surrounding walls of junk to spy out the lay of the land. Listed below are the most significant and noteworthy landmarks in Scrapwall—but keep in mind that several of these sites can be dangerous for groups freshly arrived in the region.

   Entrance (area B): This point is the only point in all of Scrapwall where there's an easily navigable gap in the surrounding ridges of junk and refuse.

   Haunted Canyon (area P): This ravine is constantly filled with a thick white mist that shrouds this spur of Scrapwall in a constant fog.

   Highest Elevation (area K): The mounds and ridges of junk and scrap surrounding Scrapwall are mostly 30 feet high, but in this region, they reach their highest elevation—50 feet. Characters who study this area for an extended period of time have a cumulative 5% chance per hour of noticing the mutant manticore that nests here coming or going from the area.

   Receiving Array (area N): A large, dish-shaped antenna rises above the ruins here, second in size only to Scrapmaster's Arena itself. The dish is 40 feet in diameter, but sits somewhat lopsided above the ridge and is streaked with rust, but at night small blinking red lights around part of its perimeter help maintain it's dominance on Scrapwall's skyline. During the day, the vultures that wheel in the sky above the array draw further attention to the location.

   Scrapmaster's Arena (area Q): This massive arena is easily the largest building in Scrapwall. Furthermore, at night, two enormous searchlights beam light into the skies above, making the arena a location that's impossible to ignore.

SCRAPWALL ENTRANCE

Scrapwall's entrance consists of a small group of buildings made from a ramshackle collection of ruins and refuse. A brief description of the areas in this complex appears below.

B1. Front Gate: A mass of metal bars, wooden timbers, and strips of refuse lashed and bolted together form a crude but effective barrier here. The gate (hardness 8, hp 50, lift DC 25, break DC 27) can be raised or lowered from area **B2** or **B6**.

B2. Guard Post: A Steel Hawks brigand is always posted here on guard duty.

B3. Observation Post: This low-ceilinged cave is only 5 feet tall. A single brigand is always posted here to watch from a hidden window in the southern wall that functions as an arrow slit. A successful DC 20 Perception check is required to notice this camouflaged gap from outside.

B4. Common Room: This room is where the brigands socialize, take their meals, or speak with newcomers to Scrapwall. At any given time, two brigands are in this room. During the day, Sevroth can be found here as well. This is where Sevroth conducts her entrance interviews with newcomers.

B5. Bunkhouse: At any given time, two brigands are resting in this room. Sevroth can be found here after dark.

B6. Storage: This large room is where the bandits store all manner of junk and supplies scavenged both from Scrapwall and from new visitors. Nothing of value is kept here at this point.

B. Entrance to Scrapwall (CR 6)

A ramshackle pair of buildings with walls and roofs made of strips of leather and fur, timbers, metal plates, and other junk lashed and bolted together sits in a gap in the surrounding mounds of refuse. Between the two buildings runs a metal gate, closed to block passage into the open area beyond.

Before the Lords of Rust claimed total dominance of Scrapwall in recent years, the Steel Hawks were the largest and most powerful of the junkyard's bandit gangs. Their leader, a ferocious and intimidating bear of a man named Varagio, gambled and lost in a conflict in the Scrapmaster's Arena against the Lords of Rust, and was killed by Kulgara in a particularly gory battle. Rather than disband the Steel Hawks, the Lords of Rust let the gang continue to exist, awarding leadership to an ex-Smiler thug named Birdfood who was only too eager to bow down before the new masters of Scrapwall, much to the shame and frustration of the surviving Steel Hawks, who view Birdfood as an interloper.

The Steel Hawks' only real responsibility today is to keep watch over the entrance to Scrapwall. Before the Lords of Rust took over, the Steel Hawks guarded this post to ensure that only exiles, criminals, and other castoffs from society were allowed into their tiny nation of junk, and that crusaders or others seeking to disrupt their way of life were turned away. Despite the upheaval in Scrapwall, all newcomers to Scrapwall must answer the Steel Hawks' questions before they're allowed to proceed onward.

The entrance is currently run by one of the Steel Hawks' two remaining officers, a short-tempered and frustrated woman named Sevroth Slaid. Angry at the current state of affairs, she hopes to depose Birdfood, seize control of the Steel Hawks, rebuild the gang's power to confront the Lords of Rust, and take back their traditional control of Scrapwall. However, she's also a realist: she knows that her combat skills pale before those of the Lords of Rust, and she has survived this long because of her acceptance of this fact. While she dutifully serves the Lords of Rust and asks the questions they require of all newcomers, she's also keeping an eye out for anyone who can help with her ambitions.

Creatures: Sevroth Slaid leads a group of a half-dozen loyal Steel Hawks here; their starting positions in the complex are noted in the Scrapwall Entrance sidebar. As soon as anyone is observed approaching the entrance, a brigand steps out of area **B2** to hail the travelers, demanding to know their business in Scrapwall; word spreads quickly throughout the complex of visitors. If the PCs attack, the bandits fight back with arrows fired from behind the gate (which provides cover) or via the narrow window in area **B3**.

Assuming the PCs don't immediately attack, Sevroth emerges from area **B4** soon after they arrive and asks them to repeat any answers they've already provided the first guard regarding their business in Scrapwall. She's really only on the lookout for errant crusaders looking for an opportunity to invade and cause trouble—as long as the PCs are respectful and not overly aggressive in demeanor, she'll give the order to open the gate. If she gets the idea that the PCs are here to take on the Lords of Rust or Hellion, she can barely contain her excitement—in any event, she invites the PCs to meet with her inside the common room (area **B4**) for what she calls a "singular opportunity to benefit us all." If the PCs refuse, she shrugs and lets them go about their business, but should the PCs later defeat Birdfood, she approaches them at some point thereafter to offer her aid in return for assurance that she'll be left in charge of the Steel Hawks when all is said and done.

When the PCs approach the entrance, they're greeted by one of the Steel Hawks guards posted here. How the guards react to the PCs depends on how they present themselves. Five likely scenarios are detailed below—use these as inspiration for reactions to other, unanticipated approaches.

Crusaders: If the PCs look like crusaders or other obvious forces of good or law and present an air of wanting to "clean out Scrapwall," they are told to turn around and leave—that Scrapwall has nothing for them. Depending on how the PCs react to this, they might be able to shift the reaction to the one described under Adventurers, below—or might incite the guards to attack.

Adventurers: This is the most likely assumption the guards make, as adventurers (or scavengers) often come to Scrapwall seeking opportunities. These groups are told that there's nothing for them in Scrapwall, but if they're looking for a place to live away from the strictures of society, they may find a new home inside. As long as the PCs don't give the impression they're here only to loot Scrapwall of anything valuable (in which case they face the same treatment as crusaders), they are instead treated as scoundrels.

Scoundrels: Most of those who come to Scrapwall are in this category—scoundrels seeking a place to call home. The guards ask potential immigrants to Scrapwall to keep their weapons stowed as they open the gate and then escort the newcomers to the Common Room (area **B4**) to answer a few questions from their commander.

Technic League: If the guards suspect the PCs are here representing the Technic League (this is unlikely unless the PCs make this bold claim themselves), they attack at once.

Members of a Scrapwall Gang: If the PCs attempt to pose as members of the Lords of Rust or another gang, they'll need to attempt Bluff and Disguise checks opposed by the guards' Sense Motive and Perception checks. If the PCs are successful, the Steel Hawks let the PCs in with no questions asked.

SEVROTH SLAID	CR 1

XP 400

Female human brawler 2 (*Pathfinder RPG: Advanced Class Guide* 23)

CN Medium humanoid (human)

Init +2; **Senses** Perception +5

DEFENSE

AC 15, touch 12, flat-footed 13 (+3 armor, +2 Dex)

hp 22 (2d10+7)

Fort +4, **Ref** +5, **Will** +0

OFFENSE

Speed 30 ft.

Melee unarmed strike +5 (1d8+2) or

flurry of blows +3/+3 (1d8+2)

Special Attacks brawler's flurry, martial flexibility 4/day

TACTICS

During Combat If the PCs attack the complex, Sevroth orders the brigands to attack the PCs at range, using the gate as cover, while she observes the fight for a few rounds. If the PCs seem to be gaining the upper hand after a few rounds, she calls for a cease-fire and invites the PCs in to speak about a truce. In a fight herself, Sevroth focuses her attacks

on the group's healers, using martial flexibility to gain Power Attack.

Morale Sevroth surrenders if brought below 8 hit points and becomes quite cooperative with the PCs; the information she can share with them is detailed in Development, below.

STATISTICS

Str 15, **Dex** 14, **Con** 13, **Int** 8, **Wis** 10, **Cha** 12

Base Atk +2; **CMB** +4; **CMD** 16

Feats Combat Expertise, Improved Unarmed Strike, Toughness, Weapon Focus (unarmed strike)

Skills Acrobatics +7, Intimidate +6, Knowledge (local) +4, Perception +5, Stealth +4, Survival +2

Languages Common, Hallit

SQ brawler's cunning, martial training

Gear mwk studded leather, 3 silverdisks, 101 gp

Sevroth Slaid

STEEL HAWKS BRIGANDS (8)	CR 1/2

XP 200 each

hp 15 each (brigand, *Pathfinder RPG NPC Codex* 266)

Development: If the PCs secure a meeting with Sevroth, she meets them in area **B4** and dismisses any other brigands there so they can talk privately. She is quick and to the point, explaining that her gang, the Steel Hawks, used to be the toughest gang in town before the Lords of Rust arrived, murdered their leader, and installed "that Smiler Birdfood" as their new commander. Sevroth rankles at this situation, but knows she's no match for the ranger and his orc minions. Her proposal to the PCs is simple—if they get rid of Birdfood so she can take control of the remnants of her gang, she'll help them however she can.

Sevroth plays things cool regarding her allegiance to the Lords of Rust. She certainly hopes the PCs are here to mix things up and take down the Lords of Rust, but she takes care to avoid giving the impression that she wants to directly oppose the powerful gang. In the short term, seizing control of the Steel Hawks is enough for her. If the PCs help her out by defeating Birdfood, she'll honor her end of the bargain and can give them information about Scrapwall's gangs—what parts of the region are under the control of which gangs, as well as the names and basic descriptions of the gangs' leaders. She can give them all of the basic information about the Lords of Rust as well, as detailed on pages 34–35 at the start of Part 3. She doesn't think to mention Dinvaya or the Clockwork Chapel on her own, but if the PCs ask about the woman, Sevroth rolls her eyes before she confirms, "Yeah, that crazy woman lives in Scrapwall. She's up in a dead-end gorge to the north, but watch out—she doesn't take well to visitors!"

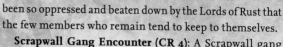

Story Award: If the PCs attack and defeat Sevroth Slaid and her eight brigands or they convince her to let them in to Scrapwall without a fight, their scrap-worth increases by 1. If the PCs forge an alliance with the Steel Hawks by defeating Birdfood for Sevroth, award them 2,400 XP in addition to the XP they would have earned defeating her and the brigands in combat (2,000 XP).

C. Steel Hawks Territory

The southernmost portion of Scrapwall is technically the territory of the Steel Hawks, but the bulk of this gang has been so oppressed and beaten down by the Lords of Rust that the few members who remain tend to keep to themselves.

Scrapwall Gang Encounter (CR 4): A Scrapwall gang encounter in this territory is with a group of six orcs, who are actually low-ranking members of the Lords of Rust more interested in menacing and tormenting lone scavengers than they are in legitimately patrolling the area. If the PCs' scrap-worth is 3 or higher, these orcs avoid conflict with them if possible.

ORCS (9)	CR 1/3

XP 135 each

hp 6 each (*Pathfinder RPG Bestiary* 222)

D. Hawk Palace (CR 6)

As with the entrance to Scrapwall, the Steel Hawks headquarters is a ramshackle structure built out of wood, bits of scrap metal, and other items of refuse scavenged from the surrounding terrain. The headquarters is now the sovereign realm of the brutal ranger Birdfood, a turncoat to the Steel Hawks placed in command of the gang by the Lords of Rust.

Creatures: Six orcs are stationed here, creatures sent by the Lords of Rust to aid Birdfood in controlling the demoralized Steel Hawks—and to keep watch on the ex-Smiler. At the first sign that Birdfood is turning against his new masters, several of these orcs are under orders to return to the Scrapmaster's Arena to inform the Lords of Rust. Birdfood himself is content with the current arrangement, and in fact is eager for the opportunity to prove his worth to the Lords of Rust, hoping to be promoted to their leadership. Defeating a band of adventurers would help his case, especially a band of adventurers who were involved in the recent events in Torch.

If the PCs attempt to approach Hawk Palace under a pretense of diplomacy, the orcs alert Birdfood at once. He emerges onto the walkway to order the visitors to hand over their weapons and magical items for "safekeeping" before coming up to the throne room (area **D5**) for their audience, at which point he and his minions attempt to capture the PCs alive to turn over to the Lords of Rust. If a fight breaks out and Birdfood is slain or captured, any surviving orcs attempt to flee back to the Scrapmaster's Arena to report the development to the Lords of Rust.

BIRDFOOD	CR 5

XP 1,600

Human ranger (beast master) 6 (*Pathfinder RPG Advanced Player's Guide* 124)

CE Medium humanoid (human)

Init +7; **Senses** Perception +10

DEFENSE

AC 18, touch 14, flat-footed 14 (+4 armor, +3 Dex, +1 dodge)

hp 55 (6d10+18)

Fort +7, **Ref** +8, **Will** +3

Birdfood

OFFENSE

Speed 30 ft.

Melee longsword +8/+3 (1d8+2/19–20)

Ranged *+1 composite longbow* +10/+5 (2d6+3/×3)

Special Attacks combat style (archery), favored enemy (elves +2, humans +4)

Ranger Spells Prepared (CL 3rd; concentration +4)

1st—*gravity bow*APG, *speak with animals*

TACTICS

Before Combat Birdfood casts *gravity bow*.

During Combat Birdfood favors ranged combat, focusing his fire on humans or elves if possible. He sends his pet hawks in to attack his targets unless he's being attacked in melee, in which case he commands them to support him by attacking anyone who attacks him, while he stays mobile to use his bow.

Morale Birdfood fights to the death.

STATISTICS

Str 14, **Dex** 16, **Con** 15, **Int** 10, **Wis** 12, **Cha** 8

Base Atk +6; **CMB** +8; **CMD** 22

Feats Dodge, Endurance, Improved Initiative, Point-Blank Shot, Precise Shot, Rapid Shot

Skills Climb +11, Handle Animal +8, Knowledge (nature) +9, Perception +10, Sense Motive +7, Stealth +12, Survival +10

Languages Common, Hallit

SQ favored terrain (plains +2), hunter's bond (hawks), improved empathic link, track +3, wild empathy +5

Combat Gear *+1 human bane arrows* (5); **Other Gear** *+1 studded leather*, *+1 composite longbow* with 15 arrows, longsword, 12 silverdisks, 109 gp

---

KIJ, REJ, AND YARKUS   CR —

Hawk animal companions (*Pathfinder RPG Bestiary* 131)

N Small animal

Init +2; **Senses** low-light vision; Perception +6

DEFENSE

AC 14, touch 13, flat-footed 12 (+2 Dex, +1 natural, +1 size)

hp 14 each (2d8+5)

Fort +4, **Ref** +5, **Will** +2

OFFENSE

Speed 10 ft., fly 80 ft. (average)

Melee bite +2 (1d4), 2 talons +2 (1d4)

TACTICS

During Combat The hawks attack whomever Birdfood commands; if he's not able to give orders, they protect his body and focus their attacks on creatures that attack them.

Morale The hawks fight to the death.

STATISTICS

Str 10, **Dex** 15, **Con** 12, **Int** 2, **Wis** 14, **Cha** 6

Base Atk +1; **CMB** +0; **CMD** 12

Feats Toughness

Skills Fly +8, Perception +6

SQ tricks (attack, come, defend, down, fetch, seek, stay)

HAWK PALACE LOCATIONS

A brief description of the locations in Hawk Palace is provided below (see the map on page 23).

D1. Walkway: At any given time, 1d4 of the orcs who serve Birdfood directly are on patrol on these wooden walkways.

D2. Storage: This room was once used for storing weapons, but the Lords of Rust have confiscated anything of value.

D3. Barracks: This room is the living quarters of the six orcs assigned by the Lords of Rust to serve Birdfood as guards (and observers, to a certain extent) . At any given time, any orcs not patrolling area **D1** can be found here, sleeping, eating, or relaxing.

D4. The Cage: Prisoners or brigands who have displeased Birdfood are kept in this reinforced chamber. The door to this room is a slab of metal that can be barred from the outside.

D5. Throne Room: This large room is split into two levels. The southern half (**D5a**) is where visitors stand while presenting their concerns, while the northern half (**D5b**) is for Birdfood himself. A large, lopsided throne made of junk and furs looms here.

D6. Birdfood's Den: Birdfood dwells here, in a room fitted with jury-rigged furniture and several stained perches for his pet hawks.

ORCS (6)   CR 1/3

XP 135 each

hp 6 each (*Pathfinder RPG Bestiary* 222)

Treasure: In addition to his gear, Birdfood has managed to keep a small stash of treasures that once belonged to now-dead Steel Hawks, trinkets and baubles the Lords of Rust allowed him to keep as part of the bribe that secured his cooperation. If the PCs defeat him and allow Sevroth to take the role as leader of the gang, she has no issues with them claiming this treasure as their own, but if the PCs offer to let her have it, she won't hesitate to take it.

The treasure is kept in area **D6**, in a dented metal locker, and consists of 234 sp, 188 gp, 11 pp, 4 silverdisks, one batteryTG, a *wand of grease* (11 charges), a *scroll of sound burst*, a masterwork hand crossbow with seven *+1 bolts*, a white access cardTG, and a timeworn fire extinguisherTG.

Story Award: If the PCs defeat Birdfood, their scrap-worth increases by 1. It increases by an additional 1 if any orcs escape back to Scrapmaster's Arena to raise the alert.

E. Unclaimed Territories

Some portions of Scrapwall are currently unclaimed by any gang—these areas, indicated on the map as area **E**, do not have Scrapwall Gang encounters associated with them. If you roll up such an encounter here, simply reroll the encounter. These areas are still inhabited by bandits and scavengers, but those who do live here maintain a low profile and generally don't travel far from their dens. They flee at the first sign of any hostility, and are generally no more than 1st-level warriors or experts.

F. The Clockwork Chapel (CR 7)

The tumultuous sound of metal grinding on metal issues forth from a constantly churning, grinding wall of gears that blocks off the western portion of this narrow valley. Only two larger gears remain motionless, situated at ground level in the center of the wall where one might expect to see a pair of doors.

This strange location is the home and chapel of one of Scrapwall's more eccentric denizens, an outcast priestess of Brigh named Dinvaya Lanalei. She's dwelled here in Scrapwall for many years, driven into hiding initially by the Technic League, but now quite comfortable in her solitude, with only her clockwork inventions to keep her company. The PCs have likely been directed to seek out Dinvaya by Joram Kyte, but she's been out of contact with civilization for some time, and getting a chance to talk to her likely requires dealing with her latest creation first (see Creatures, below).

Dinvaya Lanalei

The double doors in this chapel are immense gears that can be triggered to grind open with the flip of a hidden switch nearby. Locating a door's switch requires a successful DC 25 Perception check. Without the switch, these iron gear doors must be forced open (hardness 10, hp 60, break DC 28, Disable Device DC 30).

The wall of gears that makes up the chapel's facade at area **F1** is kept constantly wound by Dinvaya; the wall makes a lot of noise, but provides no real additional security. That said, any creature that attempts to push against the wall or interact with the gears must succeed at a DC 15 Reflex save or take 2d4 points of bludgeoning damage from the grinding gears.

Creatures: Dinvaya spends most of her time these days in her workshop (area **F5**), and does not emerge to investigate strange sounds in the outer temple. Her latest and most successful creation, a junk golem, stands guard in the central cathedral—when at rest, this construct looks like a very artistic statue of Brigh that's nevertheless cleverly crafted from junk and rubble. The golem immediately lurches to life and attacks any intruders as soon as it notices them, fighting until destroyed. Note that all the clutter and spare parts that are strewn about the entire Clockwork Chapel allow the junk golem's junk repair ability to function constantly.

Dinvaya takes notice if she hears the golem attack, but doesn't emerge from her workshop until she hears the combat end. If she finds her golem destroyed and the PCs alive, she shakes her head in disappointment, mutters, "Obviously I need to improve that thing's defenses," and then greets the PCs with eyes narrowed in suspicion. She doesn't begrudge them destroying her golem—she can always make another one—but the fact that they defeated it tells her that they're dangerous. She initially assumes the PCs are agents of the Technic League, and if their speech and actions suggest she's correct, she attacks at once, fighting to the death rather than fleeing once again. Otherwise, securing her cooperation should be relatively simple, especially if the PCs mention Joram Kyte or show her a symbol of Brigh. See page 54 for further details on how Dinvaya can help the PCs.

DINVAYA LANALEI	CR 6
XP 2,400	

hp 35 (see page 54)

JUNK GOLEM	CR 4
XP 2,400	

hp 42 (*Pathfinder RPG Bestiary 4* 132)

Story Award: If the PCs make peaceful contact with Dinvaya, award them XP as if they had defeated her in combat.

G. Smilers' Territory

The northwestern region of Scrapwall is the territory of the Smilers. These thugs are not well-loved by any of Scrapwall's denizens, but they're particularly hated by Redtooth's Raiders, with whom they are in an ongoing conflict. This conflict is somewhat ironic, as the cannibalistic Smilers aren't particularly interested in the ratfolk as a source of food. The Lords of Rust actively encourage this conflict, both for its entertainment value and because it keeps the two groups more manageable.

Scrapwall Gang Encounter (CR 5): A Scrapwall gang encounter in this territory is with four Smilers out on patrol, either looking for a lone Scrapwall denizen to abduct for dinner or hunting for ratfolk.

SMILERS (4)	CR 1
XP 400 each	

hp 19 each (see page 11)

H. Smilers' Headquarters

Unlike most of the other locations in Scrapwall, the small complex that serves as the headquarters for the Smilers is intended to be a traditional, exploration-based site. The

Smilers have far more members than can possibly dwell within the walls of this complex; most members reside in ramshackle huts or shacks spread throughout the Smilers' territory. The headquarters are built around a mostly medical facility that was once part of the larger module that crashed here long ago, a facility to which the gang's leader, a vile hobgoblin necromancer named Marrow, has taken quite a liking. The map for this location is on page 23.

The walls and doors of the headquarters are made of glaucite, an alloy of adamantine and iron (see page 18 of "Fires of Creation"). Despite its former existence as a technological laboratory, this structure lacks a power source. The sliding doors (hardness 15, hp 30, break DC 28) once opened at a touch, sliding left or right into the walls as appropriate, but without power, these doors must be wrenched open by hand. The Smilers have added scrap metal handles to the doors, but they're still difficult to open—opening a door here is a full-round action. The interior is lit by *continual flames* here and there placed long ago by Marrow.

H1. Facade (CR 4)

The ridge of refuse and junk is sheer here, like the face of a cliff. A gray metal wall sits at the base of the cliff, with a sizable metallic deck protruding south from its surface. This open-air deck is sheltered by a ragged awning of furs and scrap. Metallic double doors sit in the center of the metal wall, and above these doors protrudes a metallic armature of some sort with what appears to be a tube-shaped device fitted with a red crystal extending from the tip. A few scorch marks mar the deck's surface here and there.

The doors to the Smiler's headquarters are kept locked with a length of chain wrapped around the jury-rigged handles on the inside—a successful DC 25 Strength check is needed to wrench the doors open, or a successful DC 30 Disable Device check to slide tools through the narrow gap between the doors to disengage the chain.

Trap: Visiting Smilers know to call out their arrival before stepping up on the deck, as the armature that hangs above the door is in fact a dangerous trap—a detached robot limb with a built-in laser rifle, constructed by a now-dead tinkerer who once dwelled here. The laser rifle trap can be deactivated with the flip of a switch in area **H2**, but is currently active and set to fire upon any creature that steps up onto the deck area. The laser rifle is timeworn (*Pathfinder Campaign Setting: Technology Guide* 55) and thus prone to glitching, and only has 8 charges remaining. The trap is programmed to fire upon any target it notices, but its video sensors are failing, and it effectively has Perception +8 for the purposes of noticing targets. Each round the laser rifle turret fires, it does so on its semi-automatic setting, firing twice at the closest target each round until its charges are depleted or until no further target remains in the area.

CLOCKWORK CHAPEL LOCATIONS

Brief descriptions of the locations in the Clockwork Chapel are provided below (see the map on page 23).

F1. Clockwork Facade: The narrow valley ends at a wall of metal gears that spin and grind and turn against each other—an impressive display that does little more than make noise. A set of gear doors allows passage through the wall.

F2. Atrium: Three stone steps lead up to a pair of gear doors that open into the chapel.

F3. Chapel: This gear-shaped room contains four quite artfully carved statues of Brigh built from junk and rubble, each depicting the goddess in the act of creating a different clockwork creature—a clockwork giant spider, a clockwork boar, a clockwork lion, and a clockwork wyvern. A gear-shaped central altar sits in the middle of the room, while three regular doors allow access to other rooms. All four of these statues (not their clockwork creations) are junk golems in various stages of completion, but only the southern one is fully functional.

F4. Winding Room: This room is filled with clockwork machinery that must be wound daily to keep the noisy gear wall in area **F1** moving.

F5. Workshop: This large room is where Dinvaya builds and tinkers with her clockwork inventions.

F6. Dinvaya's Room: This room serves as a pantry, bedroom, and study for Dinvaya, although she tends to fall asleep in her workshop rather than retire to her bed here.

LASER RIFLE TURRET	CR 4

XP 1,200

Type mechanical; **Perception** DC 10; **Disable Device** DC 25

EFFECTS

Trigger visual (Perception +8); **Reset** automatic; **Bypass** switch (in area **H2**)

Effect Atk +10/+10 ranged touch (2d6 fire)

Treasure: If the trap is disarmed before the timeworn laser rifle[TG] uses the last of its 8 charges, the weapon can be salvaged.

H2. Waiting Room (CR 5)

Old wooden benches line the west and east walls of this large room. Two ruined metal tables sit in the center of the room, while a nook to the north is set off by a countertop strewn with bones and bits of junk. Two grisly chandeliers, made out of hanging bundles of skulls and bones, illuminate the room with flickering yellow flame.

A switch on the wall to the right of the southern door can be flipped to deactivate the laser rifle trap in area **H1**.

Creature: A particularly brutish member of the Smilers stands guard here—a hulking, barbaric ogrekin nicknamed "Gunshy" for his strange phobia of firearms. The ogrekin has carried this fear ever since a particularly bad incident in which a rival gang filled him full of lead (his chest is a canvas of bullet-hole scars)—he's particularly frightened by the gun turret in area **H1**.

GUNSHY	CR 5

XP 1,600

Male human ogrekin barbarian 5 (*Pathfinder RPG Bestiary 2* 204)

CE Medium humanoid (giant)

Init +5; **Senses** low-light vision; Perception +9

DEFENSE

AC 17, touch 9, flat-footed 16 (+5 armor, +1 Dex, +3 natural, –2 rage)

hp 63 (5d12+25)

Fort +10, **Ref** +2, **Will** +4; +3 vs. magic

Defensive Abilities improved uncanny dodge, trap sense +1

Weaknesses hoplophobia

OFFENSE

Speed 30 ft.

Melee *+1 greatclub* +15 (1d10+14)

Special Attacks rage (14 rounds/day), rage powers (strength surge +5, superstition +3)

TACTICS

During Combat Gunshy rages and charges at the closest foe, thrashing away with his magical greatclub. He isn't the most creative combatant, but he does enjoy making Power Attacks. Against a character who wields a firearm, he always attempts to sunder the character's weapon before attacking with intent to kill.

Morale Gunshy fights to the death unless he takes damage from a firearm while at fewer than 14 hit points. If he survives being shot at this point, he automatically attempts to flee, fighting to the death only if cornered.

STATISTICS

Str 28, **Dex** 12, **Con** 18, **Int** 8, **Wis** 13, **Cha** 6

Base Atk +5; **CMB** +14 (+16 bull rush, +16 sunder); **CMD** 23 (25 vs. bull rush, 25 vs. sunder)

Feats Improved Bull Rush, Improved Initiative, Improved Sunder, Power Attack

Skills Climb +15, Intimidate +6, Perception +9, Survival +9

Languages Common

SQ deformities (fragile, quick metabolism), fast movement

Gear *+1 hide armor, +1 greatclub*

SPECIAL ABILITIES

Hoplophobia (Ex) Gunshy's phobia of guns forces him to attempt a DC 14 Will save when confronted with firearms to avoid being shaken for 1d6 rounds. Against laser rifles, he takes a –4 penalty on this save.

Development: If combat breaks out here, the Smilers in area **H3** quickly mobilize and watch through the cracks in the door from that area for a round or so to gauge the PCs' strength. As soon as Gunshy is reduced to 20 or fewer hit points or after 5 rounds of combat (whichever comes first), these Smilers join the battle, but it takes them a full-round action to open the door.

H3. Barracks (CR 5)

The air in this room smells of smoke and burnt meat. A crude stove made of a metal barrel resting atop blocks of stone sits in the middle of an open area, while numerous doors line the walls.

The stove in the middle of the room is where the Smilers cook their meals—an investigation quickly turns up tooth-gnawed human remains tossed into the ashes in

Gunshy

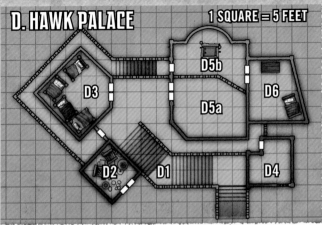

D. HAWK PALACE
1 SQUARE = 5 FEET

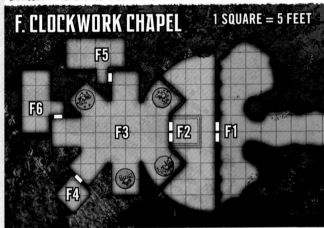

F. CLOCKWORK CHAPEL
1 SQUARE = 5 FEET

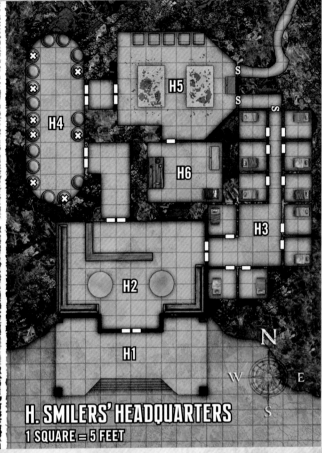

H. SMILERS' HEADQUARTERS
1 SQUARE = 5 FEET

N
W · E
S

the barrel. The secret door to the north is not particularly well-hidden—a character notices it with a successful DC 18 Perception check. Unlike the other doors in the headquarters, this door can be opened as a move action.

Creatures: This area once served as patient housing and recovery rooms for the clinic. The Smilers appointed to serve as headquarters guards by Marrow now dwell here. In all, 11 Smilers live here, but at this moment only four are present—the other seven are out hunting. If the PCs retreat and return, they may well find these other seven Smilers here on their second visit.

SMILERS (4)	CR 1

XP 400 each

hp 19 each (see page 11)

H4. Specimen Storage (CR 5)

Well over a dozen large glass tanks sit against the walls of this oval-shaped chamber. The tanks themselves are semiopaque with condensation, grit, and filth, but several of them seem to contain some sort of figure within. Each tank has a metal-rimmed door on its front allowing the contents to be accessed, and one tank to the north has been wrapped with several coils of rope.

Creatures: This chamber was once used to keep larger specimens in storage or suspended animation, pending future treatment or vivisection. The containers have not functioned in this capacity for thousands of years. Today they contain some of Marrow's more nauseating and disturbing projects—surgically altered slaves she calls her "lobotomites." Marrow has perfected a procedure to tame unruly Smilers and prisoners "lucky" enough to be spared from becoming dinner. Successfully treated patients are transformed into unintelligent drones that follow simple orders from the hobgoblin, yet have no capability to think for themselves. They know enough to eat and drink, and won't attack anyone who looks like a Smiler or Marrow, but otherwise they immediately attack any intruders with an almost feral hunger. Thematically, they function quite similarly to zombies, save that they remain living creatures.

Eight lobotomites are kept here, under orders to remain in their respective glass cages unless they see someone other than Marrow or a Smiler enter the room. The glass tanks labeled with an "X" on the map each contain one of these eight lobotomites, and as soon as anyone enters the room, the drooling thugs crack open their pens to peer out. If they don't see a Smiler or Marrow, they roar in anger and lurch forth, wielding greatclubs of bent scrap metal.

LOBOTOMITES (8) — CR 1/2

XP 200 each

Human gunslinger 1/rogue 1 (*Pathfinder RPG Ultimate Combat* 9)

N Medium humanoid (human)

Init +3; **Senses** Perception +1

DEFENSE

AC 13, touch 13, flat-footed 10 (+3 Dex)

hp 19 each (2 HD; 1d8+1d10+5)

Fort +4, **Ref** +7, **Will** +1; +2 vs. pain

DR 2/—

OFFENSE

Speed 30 ft.

Melee greatclub –2 (1d10+1)

TACTICS

During Combat Lobotomites attack the closest target with their clubs, but do not pursue foes outside of the room.

Morale A lobotomite fights to the death.

STATISTICS

Str 12, **Dex** 17, **Con** 14, **Int** —, **Wis** 13, **Cha** 1

Base Atk +1; **CMB** +2; **CMD** 15

Languages none

Gear greatclub

Development: The glass tank that's bound in coils of rope does not contain a lobotomite. Instead, it contains the latest prisoner the Smilers have capture: a ratfolk. This ratfolk isn't merely a soldier snatched from Redtooth's territory—he's that gang's beloved monster trainer and the brother of Redtooth herself, Whiskifiss.

If the PCs open this tank, they find the terrified Whiskifiss bound tightly with rope, his snout tied shut with cords. If released, Whiskifiss begs to be escorted back to Redtooth's warren (area **J**), promising all sorts of rewards to the PCs if they agree to do so. The ratfolk is grievously wounded and exhausted from hunger, but if the PCs want to seek out and defeat Marrow before escorting him home, he not only understands but eagerly encourages them to do so.

Whiskifiss's statistics below present him with all of his gear, but note that when he's first rescued he doesn't have his weapons or armor—they are currently in area **H6**.

WHISKIFISS — CR 3

XP 800

Male ratfolk ranger 4 (*Pathfinder RPG Bestiary 3* 231)

CN Small humanoid (ratfolk)

Init +4; **Senses** darkvision 60 ft.; Perception +10

DEFENSE

AC 18, touch 15, flat-footed 14 (+3 armor, +4 Dex, +1 size)

hp 38 (currently 5 hp; 4d10+12)

Fort +6, **Ref** +8, **Will** +2

OFFENSE

Speed 30 ft.

Melee short sword +4 (1d4–1/19–20)

Ranged *+1 light crossbow* +10 (1d6+1/19–20)

Special Attacks combat style (crossbow), favored enemy (constructs +2), swarming

Ranger Spells Prepared (CL 1st; concentration +2)

1st—*longstrider*

TACTICS

Before Combat Whiskifiss casts *longstrider* before entering combat if he can.

During Combat If the PCs rescue him but wish to keep fighting the Smilers, Whiskifiss cowers near the back of the party or hides during combat until he is healed up and given a few weapons. Once he's armed, armored, and healed, the ratfolk's natural bravery returns. Whiskifiss prefers to attack constructs if given the option, but otherwise favors ranged combat in battle.

Whiskifiss

Morale Whiskifiss fights to the death to protect allies or his pet rust monster (see area **J**), but he otherwise flees combat if reduced to fewer than 10 hit points.

STATISTICS

Str 8, **Dex** 18, **Con** 14, **Int** 14, **Wis** 13, **Cha** 8

Base Atk +4; **CMB** +2; **CMD** 16

Feats Deadly Aim, Endurance, Rapid Reload (light crossbow), Skill Focus (Handle Animal)

Skills Bluff +3, Climb +5, Craft (alchemy) +4, Handle Animal +9, Perception +10, Ride +10, Sense Motive +5, Stealth +14, Survival +8, Use Magic Device +1

Languages Common, Hallit, Orc

SQ favored terrain (underground +2), hunter's bond (companions), track +2, wild empathy +3

Gear studded leather, *+1 light crossbow* with 10 bolts, short sword

Story Award: If the PCs escort Whiskifiss all the way back to Redtooth's Raiders, award the PCs XP as if they had defeated Whiskifiss in combat.

H5. Surgery (CR 5)

This large chamber contains several metal tables adorned with tangles of strange devices sporting metallic, articulated arms, many of which end in blades, needles, saws, or other implements of surgery. The whole area reeks of blood and old guts, and telltale rusty brown stains besmirch the floor and walls. Lighting is provided by several burning skulls sitting here and there throughout the room.

As elsewhere in this complex, the fires that burn on the skulls are *continual flames*. A character can find each secret door in the east wall with a successful DC 18 Perception check. The northern door leads all the way through Scrapwall's outer ring of junk, providing a hidden exit to the lands beyond. The door to area **H6** is in much better condition than others in the complex, and can be opened as a move action.

Creatures: Once a surgery theater, this room is now the grisly workshop of the Smilers' necromancer leader, Marrow. Here, she makes her most vivid nightmares of flesh and metal come true. When the PCs first infiltrate the complex, Marrow is in her inner sanctum in area **H6**, but this chamber is far from unguarded. Three of her favorite creations ward the surgery—her hideous attempts to ape the cybernetic augmentations she's seen in others among the Lords of Rust. These undead are known as rust-risen, and the three cybernetic monstrosities lurch to life as soon as they note intruders in the Surgery.

RUST-RISEN (3)	**CR 2**

XP 600 each

hp 19 each (see page 90)

Development: The rust-risen are noisy when they fight, and Marrow certainly hears the sounds of conflict here. She prepares for battle in area **H6**, but if the PCs don't swiftly move on to that chamber after finishing a fight here (within 3 rounds of the end of combat), Marrow grows impatient and sends her zombie guardians north into this room, following them in and hoping to attack the PCs while the PCs are still recovering from the previous fight.

H6. Marrow's Inner Sanctum (CR 6)

This chamber combines the comforts of a cozy bedroom with the horrors of a necromantic laboratory—it's difficult to tell which pieces of furniture here are meant for relaxation and which ones are intended for torture.

Creature: The leader of the Smilers, the hobgoblin necromancer Marrow, dwells in this disturbing chamber. She keeps four zombies crafted from the remains of favorite Smilers in this room as her bodyguards and as snacks, replacing them as she noshes on them to the point where they can no longer function.

MARROW	**CR 5**

XP 1,600

Female hobgoblin necromancer 6 (*Pathfinder RPG Bestiary* 175)

NE Medium humanoid (goblinoid)

Init +3; **Senses** darkvision 60 ft.; Perception +5

DEFENSE

AC 18, touch 14, flat-footed 14 (+3 Dex, +1 dodge, +4 shield)

hp 53 (6d6+30)

Fort +6, **Ref** +6, **Will** +7

OFFENSE

Speed 30 ft.

Melee dagger +4 (1d4+1/19–20)

Special Attacks channel negative energy 5/day (DC 13)

Necromancer Spell-Like Abilities (CL 6th; concentration +8)

5/day—*grave touch* (3 rounds)

Necromancer Spells Prepared (CL 6th; concentration +8)

3rd—*hold person* (DC 15), *lightning bolt* (DC 15), *vampiric touch*

2nd—*blindness/deafness* (DC 14), *command undead* (DC 14), *daze monster* (DC 14), *ghoul touch* (DC 14), *shatter* (DC 14)

1st—*cause fear* (DC 13), *charm person* (DC 13), *magic missile* (2), *shield*

0 (at will)—*bleed* (DC 12), *light, mending, touch of fatigue* (DC 12)

Opposition Schools conjuration, illusion

TACTICS

Before Combat Marrow casts *shield* on herself.

During Combat Marrow relies on her zombies to engage the enemy in melee, allowing her to hang back and use her ranged spells on foes. She switches to her wands once her spells are exhausted, and does her best to stay mobile in a battle and out of melee entirely—her dagger is only for last resorts. She prefers to use her channeled negative energy for healing her precious undead minions.

Morale Marrow fights to the death.

STATISTICS

Str 12, **Dex** 16, **Con** 16, **Int** 15, **Wis** 8, **Cha** 10

Base Atk +3; **CMB** +4; **CMD** 18

Feats Command Undead, Craft Wand, Dodge, Iron Will, Scribe Scroll, Toughness

Skills Bluff +6, Heal +5, Knowledge (arcana) +8, Perception +5, Spellcraft +8, Stealth +7

Languages Common, Goblin, Hallit, Orc

Marrow

SQ arcane bond (dagger), power over undead

Combat Gear *potions of cure moderate wounds* (2), *wand of ray of enfeeblement* (34 charges), *wand of ray of exhaustion* (18 charges), *wand of scorching ray* (16 charges), gas grenades (2, see page 62), soothe (4 doses, see page 63); **Other Gear** dagger, *cloak of resistance +1*, 48 gp

---

HUMAN ZOMBIES (4)   CR 1/2

XP 200 each

hp 12 each (*Pathfinder RPG Bestiary* 288)

Treasure: Marrow keeps the Smilers' stash of weapons and loot here in a large metal cabinet. Within are seven batteries[TG], 22 silverdisks, a pouch of 12 fire opals worth 100 gp each, three large garnets worth 300 gp each, a case of 14 vials of soothe (see page 63), three gas grenades (see page 62), two *scrolls of animate dead*, a *scroll of command undead*, and a *scroll of technomancy*[TG]. In addition, Whiskifiss's gear (a suit of studded leather, a short sword, and a *+1 light crossbow* with 10 bolts) can be found stacked on a table near the door.

Development: If taken alive, Marrow is a font of information about Scrapwall. With her gang defeated and her power broken, she sees no point in resisting the PCs any longer and gives them any information they ask for, listlessly. Her only request is that they destroy her body completely when they're done with her so that no one brings her back as a hideous mockery of her living self, as she was so fond of doing to others. Marrow can inform the PCs about the Lords of Rust as detailed on page 35, can point out the secret escape tunnel from area H5, and can warn them of "alien undead" lurking in the easternmost portion of Scrapwall. She's tried to command these undead before to learn their secrets—she suspects they were once members of the crew of the ship that crashed here so long ago—but her one attempt to do so nearly cost her her life. She has not returned to the haunted gorge since then.

Story Award: Defeating Marrow and thus disbanding the Smilers increases the PCs' scrap-worth by 1.

I. Redtooth's Raiders Territory

This region of Scrapwall is the territory of a gang of ratfolk—Redtooth's Raiders. Once the second most powerful gang in Scrapwall, Redtooth's Raiders have fallen on hard times of late, and their territory is a mere shadow of what they once held.

Scrapwall Gang Encounter (CR 5 or 1): The first time the PCs have a Scrapwall gang encounter here, it's with a Smiler gang locked in combat with four ratfolk (with an additional 1d4 dead ratfolk strewn about the battlefield already). If the PCs aid the Smilers or simply wait for the battle to resolve itself, the Smilers turn on the PCs and attack them once the ratfolk are defeated. If the PCs aid the ratfolk, the ratfolk warily extend an offer of alliance and an invitation for a meeting with their leader, Redtooth, at area **J**.

Beyond this first encounter, additional encounters with ratfolk should be with small groups of four who prefer to spy on the PCs from places of hiding. These gangs of nervous ratfolk attack only if attacked first, and then flee as soon as one of their number is defeated or killed.

SMILERS (4)	CR 1

XP 400 each
hp 19 each (see page 11)

RATFOLK (4)	CR 1/3

XP 135 each
hp 8 each (*Pathfinder RPG Bestiary 3* 231)

J. Redtooth's Warren (CR 8)

The ratfolk of Scrapwall are led by a pragmatic but desperate creature named Redtooth (see page 60). If the PCs come upon this warren on their own, before they've been invited by Redtooth, rescued Whiskifiss, or engaged a group of ratfolk as escorts, the ratfolk guarding the warren assume the worst—that the PCs are scavengers or bandits who have come here to take advantage of the gang's hard times. In this case, the 10 ratfolk, the six dire rats, the rust monster, and Redtooth herself fight the PCs to defend their home. Convincing them that the PCs are here to talk should be difficult, especially considering that the closer the PCs get to defeating the ratfolk, the more suicidal their leader grows. Taking on the entire warren at once is a CR 8 encounter, but the ratfolk aren't interested in pursuing aggressors—if the PCs realize that they're in over their heads and flee, the ratfolk let them make their escape. Furthermore, if the PCs are defeated, the ratfolk do their best to keep the PCs alive as prisoners, so that Redtooth can try to convince them to help in return for their lives.

RATFOLK (10)	CR 1/3

XP 135 each
hp 8 each (*Pathfinder RPG Bestiary 3* 231)

DIRE RATS (6)	CR 1/3

XP 135 each
hp 5 each (*Pathfinder RPG Bestiary* 232)

CHIRPUS	CR 3

XP 800
Rust monster (*Pathfinder RPG Bestiary* 238)
hp 27

REDTOOTH	CR 5

XP 1,600
hp 8 (see page 60)

REDTOOTH'S WARREN LOCATIONS

A brief description of the locations in Redtooth's Warren is provided below (see the map on page 28).

J1. Entrance Warrens: These tunnels are 4 feet high, and Medium creatures take a –2 penalty on attack rolls and Dexterity-based checks within. Any ledges are only 2 feet high, and are treated as difficult terrain. The secret doors here can be found with a successful DC 20 Perception check.

J2. Rat Nest: The ratfolk keep six trained dire rats here as guardians—they immediately attack any intruders who are not escorted by ratfolk.

J3. Guard Room: A group of six ratfolk guard this room.

J4. Rust Monster Pen: This damp cave is where the ratfolk keep their trained rust monster, Chirpus. The creature is kept rather hungry, but holds back from attacking if Whiskifiss, whom it fears greatly, is present.

J5. Redtooth's Throne: This cave is where Redtooth meets with her subjects; her throne is made of junk and scrap metal, and is the only furnishing in the room. Four additional ratfolk stand guard here.

J6. Redtooth's Lair: The leader of the raiders lives in this cave, which is unusually clean and organized, although the individual pieces of decoration are almost universally junk (with the exception of the bits of valuable treasure detailed below in the Treasure section).

Treasure: Redtooth's Raiders once had a large amount of treasure stashed away in this warren, but they've burned through a significant portion of their stockpile in their increasingly desperate defense of their territory. All that remains of the stash now are five batteries[TG], two nanite canisters[TG], a flare gun[TG], two arc grenades[TG], a flechette grenade[TG], three zero grenades[TG], a *wand of cure moderate wounds* (18 charges), a trauma pack plus[TG], and a timeworn detonator[TG] with 4 charges. This last item is of particular importance to Redtooth; if she can find more explosives, she can to use them and this detonator to simultaneously target the Scrapmaster's Arena and the receiver array (areas **L** and **N**). Redtooth suspects more explosives can still be scavenged from the wrecked ship at area **P**, but hasn't had a chance to send out a team to look yet.

Development: If the PCs establish an alliance with Redtooth, she offers her warren as a safe house of sorts for the PCs during their time in Scrapwall. In addition, she can be a source of several quests, as detailed on page 61. Finally, if you feel that the PCs could use some backup while exploring Scrapwall, Redtooth can supply the PCs with some ratfolk to accompany them.

Story Award: If the PCs defeat Redtooth's Raiders by killing Redtooth or if they ally with Redtooth, their scrap-worth increases by 1. In addition, if they ally with the ratfolk,

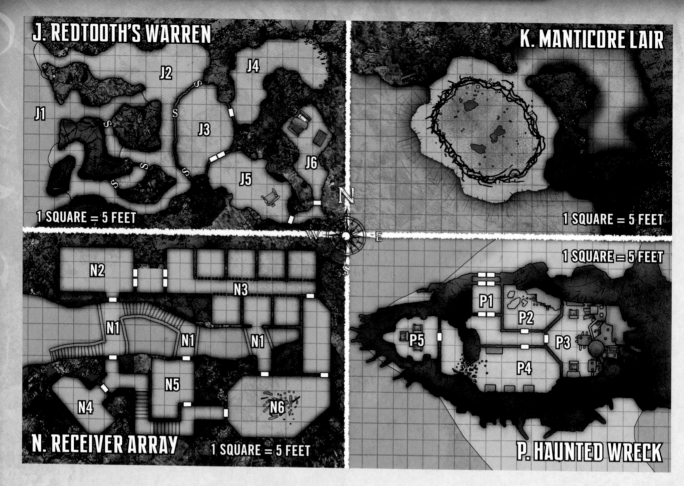

J. REDTOOTH'S WARREN

J1 · J2 · J3 · J4 · J5 · J6

1 SQUARE = 5 FEET

K. MANTICORE LAIR

1 SQUARE = 5 FEET

N. RECEIVER ARRAY

N1 · N2 · N3 · N4 · N5 · N6

1 SQUARE = 5 FEET

P. HAUNTED WRECK

P1 · P2 · P3 · P4 · P5

1 SQUARE = 5 FEET

award them 4,800 XP, less any XP the PCs may have earned in combat against the warren's defenders.

K. Manticore Lair (CR 6)

Creature: Numerous monsters and beasts dwell in the less frequented parts of Scrapwall, but the monstrous mutated manticore that dwells in this remote corner is the most ferocious. The PCs might spy the manticore flying above Scrapwall's canyons, or they could encounter it as a wandering monster at your discretion. If the PCs confront the creature in its lair, the monster fights tenaciously to defend its nest—a tangled mess of coils of razor-spiked wire, rusty chains, bones, rubble, and the like. The vicious barbs and jagged edges of the nest would certainly flense most creatures alive, but the mutant manticore's rugose hide, thickened by its years of exposure to radioactive elements, registers their touch as little more than tickles. All other creatures that move through the nest treat it as difficult terrain that deals 1d8 points of piercing and slashing damage each round (Reflex DC 15 half). If a creature has a natural armor score of +3 or higher or an armor score of +5 or higher, this damage is reduced to 1d4 points of piercing and slashing damage (Reflex DC 15 negates).

The manticore has a 50% chance of being home when the PCs arrive at the nest. If the creature isn't home when the characters arrive, it returns before they leave, perhaps attacking the PCs while they try to navigate the foul cave just beyond the monster's nest, where it tosses the mostly eaten remains of its victims.

MUTANT MANTICORE · CR 6

XP 2,400

Mutant manticore (*Pathfinder RPG Bestiary* 199, *Pathfinder Campaign Setting: Numeria, Land of Fallen Stars* 52)

LE Large aberration

Init +8; **Senses** darkvision 60 ft., low-light vision, scent; Perception +10

DEFENSE

AC 19, touch 13, flat-footed 15 (+4 Dex, +6 natural, –1 size)

hp 69 (6d10+36)

Fort +11, **Ref** +9, **Will** +5

DR 5/—; **Immune** radiation

Weaknesses vulnerable to electricity

OFFENSE

Speed 30 ft., fly 50 ft. (clumsy)

Melee bite +10 (1d8+5 plus radiation), 2 claws +10 (2d4+5)

Ranged 4 spikes +9 (1d6+5)

Space 10 ft.; **Reach** 5 ft.

TACTICS

During Combat The mutant begins combat by launching
its tail spikes, hovering over its foes while it does so. If it
hovers over its nest, the downdraft whips coils of spiky wire
and bits of sharp rubble into the air, causing any creature
affected by this effect of its Hover feat to also take 1d4
points of piercing damage each round. The manticore lands
to attack foes in melee once it uses up 12 spikes, favoring
its bite if it gets only one attack and saving its remaining
12 spikes for that day for emergencies.

Morale The mutant manticore flees, abandoning its lair and
Scrapwall forever, if reduced to fewer than 10 hit points.

STATISTICS

Str 20, **Dex** 19, **Con** 22, **Int** 5, **Wis** 12, **Cha** 7

Base Atk +6; **CMB** +12; **CMD** 26

Feats Hover, Improved Initiative, Iron Will

Skills Fly −1, Perception +10, Survival +6 (+10 when tracking);
Racial Modifiers +4 Perception, +4 Survival when tracking

Languages Common

SQ deformities (fractured mind, vulnerable to electricity),
mutations (radioactive bite, rugged)

SPECIAL ABILITIES

Mutations (Ex) The mutated manticore bears two weaknesses
as a result of its condition—a vulnerability to electricity and
a fractured mind that causes it to become confused for 1
round whenever it fails a Will saving throw. Other mutations
are beneficial to the manticore. The creature is rugged and
gains DR 5/—. Also, the radiation that affected it has become
concentrated in its fangs. Any creature it bites is exposed
to low radiation and must succeed at a DC 19 Fortitude
save or take 1 point of Constitution drain. A creature bitten
by the manticore must also succeed at a DC 19 Fortitude
save or take 1 point of Strength damage. This secondary
effect continues to plague the character until he succeeds
at two saving throws against this effect, at which point the
radiation poisoning ends. This is a poison effect; the save DC
is Constitution-based.

Treasure: The cave floor is a foul tangle of bones, grisly remains, toxic waste, and rubble—but valuable items are strewn about the place as well. Each full round of searching allows a character to attempt a DC 20 Perception check to discover one item of value. The following treasures lie hidden in the cave: a rusted iron coffer (Strength DC 15 to open) containing 250 gp, a masterwork cold iron dagger, a +1 *battleaxe*, a silver armband with inset pearls worth a total of 700 gp, a *ring of the ram* with 17 charges remaining, and an EMP pistol^TG (9 charges).

Story Award: If the PCs slay the mutant manticore, their scrap-worth increases by 1.

L. Scrapmaster's Arena

This area is covered in detail in Part 3.

M. Thralls of Hellion Territory

This region of Scrapwall was once the territory of a gang of chokers who worshiped Hellion as a god, but when the PCs disrupted the power transmission from Torch, Hellion took out his anger on this group's leaders and all but shattered the tribe. While the Thralls themselves are essentially disbanded, small groups of chokers who still venerate Hellion lurk here.

Scrapwall Gang Encounter (CR 5): A Scrapwall gang encounter in this territory is with a group of three chokers eager to earn back Hellion's favor.

CHOKERS (3)	CR 2

XP 600 each

hp 16 each (*Pathfinder RPG Bestiary* 45)

N. Receiver Array (CR 6)

Until quite recently, this site was the base of a gang of chokers who had become obsessed with the worship of Hellion, for it was here, in the twisted ruins below an immense receiver dish that was once a part of a larger communications array, that Hellion chose to first make its presence known. At that time, the complex was already the lair of a large band of chokers, and the sudden emergence of a strange voice from the very walls of their home was a shock for them. The chokers began to follow the voice's commands, and as some of their number grew devout enough, they gained the ability to cast divine spells. Thus the Thralls of Hellion were born.

Unfortunately for the chokers, Hellion chose them as the guardians of something entirely beyond their power to defend. The receiving array was where the AI had Meyanda beam power from Torch, and agents of the Lords of Rust came daily to swap out batteries and carry fully charged replacements back to the depths of the buried excavator, analogous to slowly but steadily filling an impossibly deep well. When the PCs disrupted this plan by defeating Meyanda,

the chokers panicked and tried to cover up the loss of power, but Hellion had already learned of the development. The Thralls of Hellion, its first group of devoted worshipers, became a convenient outlet for the AI's frustration and anger, and it sent the Lords of Rust to scour them from Scrapwall.

The assault occurred not long ago, and those chokers who survived are now scattered throughout the area, eager to repair the rift between themselves and their god but incapable of comprehending how to do so. The receiving array is now quiet—with no other current source of external power, it lies dormant. As the PCs explore this area, take advantage of the number of dead chokers and signs of relatively recent violence to build a sense of creeping dread—a feeling that should be heightened by signs that a new inhabitant has arrived. Any exploration of the area should turn into a game of cat and mouse as the PCs interact with the deadly alien entity that has taken up residence here.

Creatures: The bodies of the chokers who once dwelled here have been largely scavenged by a large flock of vultures that wheel in the skies above the array, yet enough half-eaten bodies remain that any visitor to the area can quickly tell that a large number of chokers once dwelled here. Many of the bodies bear crude tattoos or clutch fetishes made of junk that resemble the same robotic claw the PCs have likely seen before—Hellion's holy symbol.

The vultures do not accost visitors to the site, but a greater danger dwells within—a sinister alien entity known as a rhu-chalik. Hundreds of these small monsters infested *Divinity* thousands of years ago when the starship first clashed with the Dominion of the Black, and the alien aberrations have taken to life on Golarion quite well. This particular rhu-chalik dwells in area **N6**, but once it notices PCs in the area, it begins stalking them. Give this cat-and-mouse encounter an air of brooding, creeping horror—the rhu-chalik may even stalk the PCs for hours only to attack once they bed down for the night. Although this rhu-chalik is a native of Golarion and has never known the company of other creatures from the Dominion of the Black, it still feels a mental connection to that realm—while it doesn't fully understand its urge to transmit the memories of its victims into the dark places between the stars, it enjoys the process immensely. Keep track of any PCs who have their thoughts and memories duplicated and transmitted in this manner, as it may have repercussions in Part Four, "Valley of the Brain Collectors."

RHU-CHALIK	CR 6

XP 2,400

hp 68 (see page 86)

Development: If the PCs are sent here by Redtooth to destroy the receiver array, by placing a cylex charge on the dish's support structure, the PCs will first need to succeed at a DC 15 Knowledge (engineering) check to determine the most strategic point on the building to place the charge—make this check in secret so the PCs don't know whether they were successful or not. It's a 20-foot climb to reach the support structures (Climb DC 15), at which point a character must succeed at a DC 10 Disable Device check to place and arm the explosive. Remember, working with technological explosives in this way carries penalties for characters who don't have the Technologist feat! Once the explosive is set, the PCs need only trigger it using the detonator—if the charge was improperly set with a failed Knowledge (engineering) check, the explosion is loud and flashy, but it doesn't destroy the receiver and the charge of cylex is wasted. The PCs can try again if they have enough cylex; in any event, the array automatically collapses (and buries areas **N1** through **N6** in the process) after three such attempts.

Story Award: If the PCs destroy the array, award them 1,200 XP and their scrap-worth increases by 1.

O. Haunted Canyon

This region of Scrapwall is constantly shrouded with strange mists that obscure all sight beyond 5 feet. The mists are clammy and unpleasant, and radiate faint necromancy—they are a direct result of the haunting presence, locked within a wrecked ship deeper in the canyon (area **P**). If the PCs destroy the undead that dwell in area **P**, the mists in this canyon lift forever.

As long as these mists persist, the channel resistance of all undead and haunts encountered here and in the wreck (area **P**) is increased to +4 (this does not stack with any existing channel resistance).

Scrapwall Gang Encounter (CR 4): A Scrapwall gang encounter in this territory is with a group of four poltergeists. The poltergeists that haunt this canyon have a wider range of movement than most poltergeists, but they cannot leave the fog-shrouded area, and if the fog lifts, the poltergeists that haunt the canyon vanish as well.

POLTERGEISTS (2)	CR 2

XP 600 each

hp 16 each (*Pathfinder RPG Bestiary 2* 211)

P. Haunted Wreck

The source of the unnatural mist and the poltergeists that haunt this canyon is a crashed scout ship lodged deep in the ravine's easternmost end. Despite the thick, clammy mist, any who delve deep enough into the ravine are certain to stumble upon the ruins of the ship as they reach the end of the fissure. This crashed ship was originally launched as a last-ditch effort by the doomed recycling module's crew to escape death. They made it only to the very edge of the crash

---

RECEIVER ARRAY LOCATIONS

Brief descriptions of the locations below the Receiver Array are provided below (see the map on page 28).

N1. Rickety Walkways: These wooden walkways sway alarmingly if a Medium or larger creature walks on them, but they are strong and can support such creatures' weights with ease. The walkways vary in height from 10 feet to 20 feet.

N2. Guard Post: Once a place for the chokers to stage and organize the defense of the complex, this room is now empty.

N3. Old Dens: These rooms once served as barracks for the chokers—they're abandoned now.

N4. Holding Chamber: Any PCs captured by the thralls of Hellion are locked into this room; the door is made of glaucite (hardness 15, hp 30, break DC 28, Disable Device DC 30).

N5. Power Uplink: The batteries for harvesting and storing the power broadcast to the receiver array were once kept here, but they've been relocated to area **R4**.

N6. Rhu-Chalik Den: Once a temple devoted to Hellion, this room is now in ruins. Fragments of the statue of a man-sized, clawed hand (similar to the one the PCs found in the previous adventure) have been gathered together to form a nest for the array's current denizen, a monstrous alien known as a rhu-chalik.

---

site before being engulfed in the devastation. Having met their end in the throes of fear and despair, and still under the influence of the Dominion of the Black's madness-inducing weaponry, the doomed crew persist to this day as undead.

Much of the wrecked ship lies buried under rubble, but its starboard airlock hatch is clear of rubble—its glaucite doors hang open, revealing area **P1** within. The ship is made of glaucite, and sits at an awkward angle on the ground, tilted downward from aft to stern at a noticeable angle. This, combined with the amount of rubble and junk strewn across the floors, turns the ground within the wreck into difficult terrain.

Ceiling height inside the wreck remains a constant 8 feet, and there is no illumination. All of the doors in the wreck, with the exception of the one to area **P5**, are opened and in the absence of power, it cannot be closed without considerable effort—power cannot be restored to the wreck in any event.

P1. Airlock

The air is unnaturally cold in this empty atrium. Metal doorways yawn to the north and south, and the slanted floor is strewn with strange bits of rubble and twisted lengths of metal. The ceiling is badly damaged here, its gray metal shell shattered in numerous places, exposing coils of rusty, mold-covered cables and wires.

The wreck's airlock and central corridor are devoid of threats, yet as soon as any PCs set foot in the ruins, the presence of their living bodies rouses the undead energies suffusing the area. The doors to areas **P2** to **P4** all hang open. From area **P2** comes a soft grinding sound, like that of metal scraping against metal. From area **P3** a faint light, similar to that of a lantern held aloft, casts strange, flickering shadows through a tangle of rubble. And from area **P4** issues the cloying stink of rotted flesh.

Development: The denizens of the neighboring areas are dangerous, but fortunately, they do not gang up on the PCs at first. The poltergeists in area **P2** emerge as soon as any sound or new source of light comes into this area, attacking within 1d3 rounds if the PCs don't first enter another room. The will-o'-wisp in area **P3** hangs back until it's attacked or no undead remain in the wreck. The skeletal champions in area **P4** remain dormant until the PCs awaken them as detailed in that area.

P2. Cargo Bay (CR 5)

The northeastern wall of this blasted chamber was obviously super-heated at some point, for here and there, the walls ran waxlike, forming slag that cooled into puddles of steel all along the floor. Debris litters the floor—it might once have been tech of great value but now is mere scraps of unsalvageable, half-melted junk.

This small hold was once where the scout ship stored cargo, gear, and emergency supplies. The northeastern wall suffered the brunt of the ship's crash, but not all of the supplies kept here were completely destroyed.

Creatures: A trio of poltergeists formed from the ambient horror and fear of those who died during the ship's crash, and still linger on here. The malevolent spirits quickly attack any intruders, hurling fragments of rubble and old gear around with their telekinesis. Some of these objects include a few remaining charges of cylex—fortunately, the explosives are stable enough that such treatment won't detonate them. The same is not true of the grenades found here—each round a poltergeist makes an attack with its telekinesis, there's a 10% chance it does so by hurling one of the three grenades found in the room, causing it to explode upon impact. If any of the poltergeists use their frightener ability, they appear as humans dressed in damaged spacesuits, with missing limbs, shattered face plates, and swaths of flesh scorched away by blasts of fire.

Once all of the undead in the wreck are destroyed, these poltergeists no longer rejuvenate.

POLTERGEISTS (3)   CR 2
XP 600 each
hp 16 each (*Pathfinder RPG Bestiary 2* 211)

Treasure: Amid the clutter in this chamber are 43 silverdisks, a timeworn grenade launcher[TG] (14 charges), three concussion grenades[TG], a timeworn emergency beacon[TG] (18 charges), a timeworn emergency raft[TG] (3 charges), a timeworn emergency shelter[TG], and 3 charges of cylex[TG].

P3. Engine Room (CR 6)

The eastern half of this room is a tangle of gray metal, strange engine parts, and rubble, all of which was subjected to great heat long ago, judging by the metal's melted and scorched surfaces. Here and there, softly glowing residues are caked onto bits and pieces of the metal.

This was once the ship's engine room—the ruins of the machinery are the remains of its destroyed fusion reactor. The explosion resulting from the vehicle's crash obliterated most of the back half of the ship while leaving what remains damaged and ruined. Three patches of glowing chemical residue cake the ruined reactor—consuming any of these three patches can have strange effects (see Numerian Fluids on page 28 of *Numeria, Land of Fallen Stars*).

Creature: A single will-o'-wisp has taken up residence here, feeding upon the self-sustaining ambient horror and distress left behind by the long dead crew. As delicious as the undead's torment may be, though, the will-o'-wisp prefers the fear and despair of the living, and as the PCs begin to explore the wreck, the will-o'-wisp becomes invisible and stalks them. If the PCs sneak up on it first, they find it flitting and floating among the rubble here, chasing invisible and intangible motes of sadness through the air. If caught in this way, it immediately becomes invisible, attacking only if the PCs do so first.

Once all of the undead are slain and the haunt plaguing the region is lifted, the will-o'-wisp attacks the PCs out of anger. It fights until reduced to 20 or fewer hit points, at which point it flees Scrapwall to find a new home.

WILL-O'-WISP   CR 6
XP 2,400
hp 40 (*Pathfinder RPG Bestiary* 277)

P4. Stasis Pods (CR 5)

The air in this compartment is choking and stale. The dust here is inches thick—nothing has disturbed this area in years. To the west, the wall is partially crushed and melted, leaving a five-foot-wide, two-foot-tall gap that opens into another chamber beyond. Four large coffin-shaped objects made of glass and metal sit against the walls—one to the north and three to the south. The northern pod and the central southern pod are partially broken. Each contains a skeleton clad in fragments of strange, bulky armor. The other two southern pods appear to be only slightly damaged. The air is thick with a rancid scent, like old meat gone bad.

The pods in this chamber were used by crew members of the scouting ship for stasis sleep on long journeys. When the ship's captain originally attempted to escape the crashing module, four technicians donned space suits and entered these pods for safety, but that protection wasn't enough—all four died on impact. Two of the pods broke open, and the remains within are now only crumbling bones, but in the other two pods, the bodies of the crew remain in perfect stasis in their pristine space suits. One is male, the other female—both appear to be human, yet of an unknown ethnicity with dusky skin, reddish hair, and delicate features. The pods they rest in seem to be intact, but in fact failed long ago as well—their remains are held together by necromantic energies, not technology. Any attempt to open one of these pods is automatically successful, but causes the pod to shatter and crumble away into the same state of disrepair as the others.

Creatures: If any of the remains in this room or any of the pods in which they lie are disturbed, the undead spirits within the room immediately animate the remains with howls of wrath. Before this point, the air quality in the room was poor, but when the undead rise, the stink increases as both of the apparently intact bodies rise up and swiftly decay, flesh and spacesuit alike, until what stands before the PCs are two animated skeletons clad in destroyed spacesuits. The undead spirits within the ship attempt to animate the other two skeletal remains as well, yet as they rise up, time takes its toll and the bones crumble to dust, leaving only two skeletal champions to attack the PCs.

In this first round of combat, the air in the room becomes cloying enough that every creature in area **P4** must succeed at a DC 15 Fortitude save or be nauseated for 1d4 rounds.

attack the PCs, and pursue the PCs relentlessly if they flee, even beyond the boundaries of Scrapwall.

Morale These undead fight until destroyed.

STATISTICS

Str 14, **Dex** 11, **Con** —, **Int** 16, **Wis** 11, **Cha** 10
Base Atk +4; **CMB** +6; **CMD** 16
Feats Alertness, Armor Proficiency (Medium, Heavy), Improved Initiative, Improved Natural Attack[B] (claw)
Skills Diplomacy +6, Disable Device −7, Intimidate +5, Knowledge (engineering) +12, Knowledge (geography) +12, Perception +11, Profession (navigator) +9, Sense Motive +11, Survival +6
Languages Androffan
Gear ruined space suit[TG]

Skeletal Technician

SKELETAL TECHNICIANS (2)	**CR 3**

XP 800 each
Human skeletal champion expert 4 (*Pathfinder RPG Bestiary* 252)
NE Medium undead
Init +4; **Senses** darkvision 60 ft.; Perception +11

DEFENSE

AC 15, touch 10, flat-footed 15 (+3 armor, +2 natural)
hp 31 each (6 HD; 2d8+4d8+4)
Fort +1, **Ref** +3, **Will** +7
Defensive Abilities channel resistance +4; **DR** 5/bludgeoning; **Immune** cold, undead traits

OFFENSE

Speed 20 ft.
Melee 2 claws +6 (1d6+2)

TACTICS

During Combat The skeletal technicians use their talons to

Treasure: The two space suits worn by the undead are ruined, but they still grant a small armor bonus if worn. They effectively have the broken condition and offer none of the protection from energy, radiation, or vacuum that a functional space suit grants, essentially reducing them to bulky, heavy armor with prohibitive armor check penalties and poor protection values. Nonetheless, the four curious suits are worth 200 gp each to collectors for their novelty alone. Among the remains in the four pods are four gray access cards^TG.

P5. Bridge (CR 6)

The door to this chamber, unlike the other doors in the wreck, is closed. With no power supply, the glaucite door must be either smashed opened or coaxed open with a successful Disable Device check (hardness 15, hp 30, break DC 28, Disable Device DC 30). When the door is opened, a blast of stale, foul-smelling air hisses out of the chamber.

A massive black window, spiderwebbed with hundreds of cracks, graces the western wall of this chamber, half-buried under rubble and twisted metal. Curved consoles of strange controls line the walls, with three chairs made of an unidentifiable off-white material facing them. A figure dressed in red fabric of an unusually fine weave sits slumped over the console in the westernmost chair.

The remains seated in the pilot's station are those of Captain Yurian Valako, once the captain of *Divinity*'s recycling module. As fresh air fills the bridge, his remains, which had mummified, slump and slowly crumble away until nothing remains but a few brittle bones and a pile of dust within his armor. As this takes place, each PC in the vicinity becomes suddenly overwhelmed with a series of powerful visions—flashes of emotion mixed with the sound of screaming and explosions, sudden feelings of vertigo, and the conviction that gravity has gone mad. Each PC must succeed at a DC 14 Will save or fall prone and be staggered for 1 round as she experiences the hell and chaos of the crash. The vision passes quickly, but in its wake comes something far more dangerous—Yurian's unquiet shade.

Creature: As his body crumbles away, Yurian's soul rises up from his remains in a seething vortex of shadows and crimson dust, coalescing into a vaguely humanoid shape with long, thin fingers that wisp away into smoke. As he manifests as an advanced wraith, Yurian cries out in despair and pain as he drifts forward to attack. Once awakened in this manner, Yurian fights until destroyed and pursues foes throughout the wreck, but not beyond into the surrounding mists. If the PCs return at a later date, the wraith seeks them out as soon as he notices their arrival; he does not wait for victims to return to the bridge to attack.

YURIAN VALAKO	CR 6

XP 2,400
Advanced wraith (*Pathfinder RPG Bestiary* 281, 294)
hp 57

Treasure: Yurian's sidearm, a timeworn mind burner (9 charges, see page 63) sits on the floor to the right of his remains; the red scatterlight suit^TG he wore is in excellent condition. Amid the dust of his remains inside the suit is an envoy's mouthpiece (see page 62) and a well-preserved and fully functional piece of cybertech: a skillslot^TG. Any attempt to examine the envoy's mouthpiece triggers its playback feature, causing it to play the following short message, spoken in Androffan—this message repeats each time the playback button is pressed.

"This is the final report of salvage module *Chrysalis*, Captain Yurian Valako reporting. *Divinity* is lost; the rest of the ship's crew is presumed dead or worse. The surviving crew of *Chrysalis* and I are boarding a launch and will attempt an emergency landing, but without AI control, the prospects of a safe landing are minimal. I've secured an inhibitor facet—if I can install it into the Unity interface, it should disable the AI's security long enough for us to reclaim control and perhaps even signal for help from home. I'm boarding the launch now, and will append further reports after our successful landing."

Although the PCs may not immediately realize it, the most valuable of Yurian's treasures is tucked away in one of the pockets of his scatterlight suit—the inhibitor facet (see page 63) mentioned in his mouthpiece recording. It's a resource the PCs can use against Hellion in area **S3**, and can use it again at the end of the Adventure Path to shape the abilities and personality of a new god of their own design (see "The Divinity Drive").

Story Award: If the PCs exorcise the canyon by slaying all of the undead in this wreck, their scrap-worth increases by 1. In addition, if the PCs translate the message on the mouthpiece, award them 1,600 XP for discovering this information.

PART 3: HELLION'S DOMAIN

The immense battlefield known as Scrapmaster's Arena is the eventual goal of the PCs, for it is below this large fighting pit that Hellion is hidden away within the buried excavator it hopes to someday awaken and inhabit. Wise PCs do not immediately attempt to lay siege to or invade the mad AI's domain, for until the PCs build up their local reputation, the AI's minions, the Lords of Rust, keep the area under tight control.

The PCs can learn about Hellion and the Lords of Rust by speaking to other NPCs throughout Scrapwall. Listed below is information about the gang, its leaders, and Hellion that is common knowledge. How much of this information the PCs can learn from a given NPC is left largely to you, but they should know all of this information by the time they decide to begin the assault on the arena and its buried fortress.

Lords of Rust: This gang comprises a motley group of creatures, but the majority are orcs, androids, and ratfolk. The bulk of these gang members dwell in the rubble and ruins throughout the Lords of Rust territories or in the nooks and crannies of Scrapmaster's Arena—few actually live in the gang's headquarters, but as long as the Lords of Rust remain dominant and the PCs don't threaten them, these low-ranking members will certainly rush to bolster the headquarters' defenses. In all, the Lords of Rust number several hundred strong.

Scrapmaster's Arena: Every few days, the Lords of Rust invite those who have caught their attention to audition for membership in the gang. Such auditions consist of fights in Scrapmaster's Arena, usually against groups of gang members or captured monsters, but sometimes against the troll Helskarg herself. Those who survive these fights are granted membership in the gang, while those who don't are generally eaten. The arena fights are known to be unfair and cruel.

Draigs: The ettin Draigs wields two spiky chains with unnerving grace in combat. She's the thug and executioner for the leadership—the one Hellion calls upon to mete out punishment to those who sin against Hellion.

Helskarg: The troll Helskarg is a garrulous creature and something of the front face of the Lords. She guards the entrance to the gang's lair, but more importantly, she orchestrates the fights in the Scrapmaster's Arena.

Kulgara: After Meyanda's loss, Kulgara seized control of the gang as its commander, and now ranks just under Hellion. She increasingly sees the Lords of Rust as her own gang.

Meyanda: This android was once the high priestess of Hellion and the leader of the Lords of Rust, and her loss has thrown the gang into disarray—though none outside of the gang miss her cruelty. Her leadership duties have been split between Kulgara and Nalakai.

Nalakai: With the loss of Meyanda, Nalakai is the most powerful cleric of Hellion remaining in Scrapwall. Vexed by Kulgara's cocky attitude and growing hunger for power, Nalakai hopes to find proof that Kulgara intends to betray Hellion so that he can engineer her demise and replace her in the role of commander of the Lords of Rust.

Zagmaander: The most mysterious Lord of Rust is the crimson-skinned monster Zagmaander, who is something of a local bogeyman. Zagmaander serves Hellion as an enforcer and assassin, and even the other Lords of Rust leaders fear her.

Hellion: Hellion is the lord and god of the Lords of Rust. Many have heard its voice or have seen its fiendish visage on the monitors found throughout the excavator, yet none can say they've seen Hellion in the flesh. Most believe Hellion to be a powerful fiend (a demon or devil), while others suspect it of being a Technic League agent using a fiend's facade to sow fear. Others believe it to be an alien, the ghost of an ancient crew member from the Silver Mount, or even a trickster posing as a god. None have yet come close to the truth.

Scrap-Worth Repercussions

The following encounter areas present the Lords of Rust headquarters with the assumption that the PCs have achieved the maximum scrap-worth score of 10, and in doing so have put the Lords of Rust on high alert and on the defensive. While this means that the Lords are expecting the PCs, it also means that many of their lower-ranking minions flee in the face of what appear to be superior foes in the PCs, resulting in far fewer enemies to fight overall. If the PCs attempt to attack the headquarters before their scrap-worth reaches 10, they'll find its defense bolstered by numerous additional orcs, ratfolk, cultists of Hellion, and other creatures. Each time the PCs defeat one of the leaders of the Lords of Rust, their scrap-worth increases by 1.

The additional gang members present in the headquarters at lower scrap-worth tiers are composed of a mix of chokers, Smilers, ratfolk, orcs, acolytes of Hellion, and human brigands. Mix and match these guards as you wish to increase the CR of encounters as directed below, but keep in mind that if the PCs have accomplished certain goals in Scrapwall, some choices may no longer be available to the Lords of Rust as guards, regardless of the PCs' overall scrap-worth. Orcs and human brigands are always available to the Lords of Rust as reinforcements.

Scrap-Worth 10: This is the maximum value of scrap-worth attainable. At this level, all of the additional resources that would normally be available to defend the headquarters abandon their duties, leaving the defense solely to the leadership and their most loyal of followers, as presented on the following pages.

Scrap-Worth 8–9: The Lords of Rust have additional guards to protect them in their individual encounters—add enough additional guards to these encounters to raise their CR by 1. For example, the encounter with the ettin Draigs is normally a CR 7 encounter, but in this case you'd add enough chokers, Smilers, ratfolk, Scrapwall brigands, and orcs to increase the encounter to a CR 8 encounter (thus, any combination of guards worth a total of 1,600 XP in all—two chokers and two brigands, for example, or perhaps four Smilers).

Scrap-Worth 4–7: Bolster encounters with the Lords of Rust as detailed above. In addition, add 8 additional CR 4 encounters with gang members to various rooms of your choice throughout the complex. These additional encounters can be replaced on a daily basis until the PCs' scrap-worth reaches 8 or higher.

Scrap-Worth 1–3: Bolster encounters with the Lords of Rust and add 8 additional CR 4 encounters with gangs as detailed above. In addition, every level of Hellion's domain save the lowest gains a CR 3 patrol of guards led by a single dark slayer (making the entire patrol encounter a CR 5 encounter). The PCs should encounter this patrol at some point while exploring that level, but before they get too far in. These patrols can be replaced on a daily basis until the PCs' scrap-worth hits 4 or higher.

Scrap-Worth 0: As the situation for Scrap-Worth 1–3 above, save that all of the headquarters' occupants have excellent morale and gain a +2 bonus on all attack rolls, saving throws, and skill checks.

Acolyte of Hellion

DARK SLAYER — CR 3
XP 800 each
hp 22 each (*Pathfinder RPG Bestiary 2* 75)
Special Dark slayers appear as leaders for patrols, but only if the PCs' scrap-worth is 3 or lower.

CHOKERS — CR 2
XP 600 each
hp 16 each (*Pathfinder RPG Bestiary* 45)
Special If the PCs destroy the receiver array above area **N**, the remaining chokers in Scrapwall go to ground, and none are available to bolster defenses here.

SMILERS — CR 1
XP 400 each
hp 19 each (see page 11)
Special No Smilers are available to bolster numbers here if the PCs have slain Marrow and thus disrupted her gang.

RATFOLK — CR 1/3
XP 135 each
hp 8 each (*Pathfinder RPG Bestiary 3* 231)
Special A day after the PCs ally with Redtooth, word spreads far enough that the ratfolk among the Lords of Rust abandon the gang. In this event, no ratfolk are available to bolster defenses in the headquarters.

ORCS — CR 1/3
XP 135 each
hp 6 each (*Pathfinder RPG Bestiary* 222)

ACOLYTES OF HELLION — CR 1/2
XP 200
Human cleric of Hellion 1
CE Medium humanoid (human)
Init +0; **Senses** Perception +3

DEFENSE
AC 17, touch 12, flat-footed 17 (+4 armor, +2 deflection, +1 shield)
hp 13 (1d8+5)
Fort +3, **Ref** +0, **Will** +4

OFFENSE
Speed 30 ft.
Melee spiked gauntlet +3 (1d4+3)
Special Attacks channel negative energy 4/day (DC 11, 1d6)
Domain Spell-Like Abilities (CL 1st; concentration +3)
  5/day—artificer's touch, vision of madness
Cleric Spells Prepared (CL 1st; concentration +3)
  1st—*cure light wounds, lesser confusion*ᴰ (DC 13), *shield of faith*
  0 (at will)—*bleed* (DC 12), *mending, stabilize*
  D domain spell; **Domains** Artifice, Madness

TACTICS
Before Combat An acolyte of Hellion casts *shield of faith*.

During Combat The acolytes save *lesser confusion* to use against ranged foes and casts *cure light wounds* on themselves as soon as possible after being wounded, but otherwise focus their attacks with their gauntlets on foes. An acolyte uses her channel negative energy if surrounded (without care to any allies who might be hit by the effect).

Morale An acolyte fights to the death.

STATISTICS

Str 16, **Dex** 10, **Con** 13, **Int** 8, **Wis** 15, **Cha** 12

Base Atk +0; **CMB** +3; **CMD** 15

Feats Power Attack, Toughness

Skills Knowledge (religion) +3, Perception +3

Languages Common, Hallit

Gear chain shirt, light steel shield, spiked gauntlet, 20 silverdisks

Story Award: If the PCs' scrap-worth reaches 10, award them 4,800 XP.

EXCAVATOR FEATURES

The bulk of the Lords of Rust headquarters is found within the partially buried chambers of an immense excavator. Only a portion of the excavator's interior has been dug up so far—Hellion's madness has slowed the rate of progress in uncovering the device, as has its desire to free it carefully, without causing further subsidence that could rebury or damage it. Until the excavator is fully powered, in any event, the AI sees little need to hasten the process. An illustration of the excavator itself as it would appear once it has fully emerged from the ground appears on the inside front cover of this book.

Although most of the excavator remains buried, the device's engines have been charged enough to supply power to most of the chambers within the buried vehicle. The ceiling height in the excavator's cabin and halls is a uniform 11 feet. Lighting is provided by glowing panels high on the walls or on the ceiling, and can be controlled by touching a wall-mounted panel as a move action to vary a room's illumination between darkness and bright light. The walls, doors, ceilings, and floors are all made of glaucite (hardness 15, hp 30 per inch), and the windows are made of strengthened polymers that are as transparent as glass but share glaucite's hardness and hit points. The doors (hardness 15, hp 15, break DC 28, Disable Device DC 35) are made of horizontal glaucite slats that fold upward like an accordion when opened, and slide up into a slot in the top of the door's frame. A door can be opened or closed by touching a panel next to the door as a swift action—opened doors close automatically at the end of a round unless an object blocks the doorway. All of the doors in the excavator can be locked, and when they're locked, a successful DC 35 Disable Device check is required to open them (characters without the Technologist feat take a penalty on such checks). A gray or better access card (such as those found in area **P4**) can unlock and open these doors with a touch as a swift action.

Hellion infuses the entirety of the excavator. The AI first arrived here inside of a large arachnid robot (see area **T3**), but today its awareness extends throughout the excavator as well. The AI's primary link to the excavator is in area **S3**; as long as the computers remain powered and functional there, it retains the ability to observe and speak through the security monitors placed throughout the complex, which are indicated on the map, and the AI automatically attempts Perception checks to notice the PCs when they come into range of the monitors' built-in audio and visual sensors (these sensors work as well as human sight and hearing, but also possess low-light vision and darkvision with a range of 60 feet). Hellion cannot take direct action against the PCs in these areas unless otherwise indicated in the text, but it can certainly speak to and taunt them or raise alarms.

Note that certain underground portions of the headquarters (areas **S7** through **S12** and areas **T1** through **T3**) are not within the excavator but rather are built in natural caverns. In these areas, the ceiling height averages 7 feet in tunnels and 12 feet in caves unless otherwise noted. The chambers are generally lit by external lights from portions of the excavator that extend from the cave walls.

Hellion Monitors

Throughout the complex, Hellion can observe and interact via a linked network of sensors and monitors (hardness 5, hp 10, break DC 20). Each of these monitors appears as a rectangular glass panel set into a wall. Each panel measures 2 feet wide and 18 inches tall, and features hidden sensors that grant Hellion sight, low-light vision, darkvision to a range of 60 feet, and hearing. Hellion is capable of observing through any number of these monitors simultaneously, and can control the imagery of the monitor somewhat—it prefers to manifest as a demonic face, and to speak with a deep, rumbling voice devoid of emotion. It is via these monitors that Hellion communicates with its worshipers, and as the PCs explore the excavator, it is via these monitors that the AI taunts and torments them.

Hellion can use any of these monitors as a conduit for its spell-like abilities (see page 56), but can do so only once per minute. The following encounters note the points at which Hellion prefers to use its spell-like abilities, but you can adjust these as you see fit. But Hellion's primary use for these monitors should be to interact with the PCs, taunting and teasing them as they delve deeper into its domain. From a metagame perspective, these taunts should not only help to build up the tension and encourage the PCs to seek out the evil AI for a final confrontation, but also foreshadow future events in the Iron Gods Adventure Path or even to inform the PCs of key pieces of information. It is through these taunts from Hellion, for example, that the PCs are likely

Hellion Monitor

seats—a raucous mix of orcs, ratfolk, and humans eager to see blood spilled.

Creatures: If the PCs are invited by Helskarg to take part in the Scrapmaster's Arena and they take up the offer, the resulting fight gives the PCs a chance to give their scrap-worth a final boost in full view of the public. The PCs are allowed to bring whatever they wish to the fight, which takes place in the arena. The majority of the gang surrounds the battlefield—hundreds of orcs and ratfolk, with a scattering of humans and others, all eager to see the bloodshed. When the PCs arrive, Helskarg reveals that she has decided to face them herself—or more accurately, with her two pet ogres from area **Q3**. The troll fights in a jury-rigged chariot drawn by the two ogres, and until she realizes the PCs are putting up a significant fight, she spends as much time bragging and showing off to the audience as she does actually attacking the PCs. Rules for chariots in combat appear on pages 170–187 of *Pathfinder RPG Ultimate Combat*; Helskarg's ogre-drawn chariot functions as a heavy chariot (*Ultimate Combat* 182, but not armed with a ballista), and she uses Intimidate checks rather than Handle Animal checks for her driving checks.

If, on the other hand, the PCs come to the arena uninvited (or arrive before their scheduled fight is to take place), they find the arena to be relatively deserted. At your discretion, the PCs might encounter a few orcs sparring in the battlefield, but they immediately flee toward area **Q2** and call out to Helskarg if confronted. In this case, Helskarg leaps off the balcony to attack the unwelcome guests, presenting a less deadly encounter than when she's got her ogres at hand, but also decreasing the potential scrap-worth award for her defeat.

to first learn the name of the crashed ship and about the oracle Casandalee, and to hear that an even greater danger, Unity, dwells within Silver Mount.

As the PCs delve deeper and learn more about Hellion, they'll likely have questions. Hellion is assured of its superiority, so it often answers questions posed to it when it contacts the PCs via these monitors. See Hellion's writeup on page 86 for likely questions and answers.

Story Award: If the PCs destroy all of the monitors in the excavator, award them 1,200 XP.

Q1. Scrapmaster's Arena (CR 8)

An enormous battlefield sprawls here—a fighting arena that measures several hundred feet in diameter, ringed by mounds of junk and refuse stacked in tiers for seating. The ring has an arched opening in its westernmost end to allow access to the arena, while against the eastern side, a large metallic structure akin to a squat tower protrudes from the hard-packed earth. A wooden stairway wraps around the tower's sides, and a twenty-foot-tall stage protrudes from its western facade, overlooking the arena below.

The arena measures 400 feet in diameter; it's a roughly circular area of open ground with low mounds of junk scattered about in order to break up the battlefield and provide cover. Normally, the ring is unoccupied, but during fights, the bulk of the Lords of Rust's members fill the

HELSKARG	CR 7

XP 3,200

Female troll fighter 2 (*Pathfinder RPG Bestiary* 268)

CE Large humanoid (giant)

Init +4; **Senses** darkvision 60 ft., low-light vision, scent; Perception +4

DEFENSE

AC 20, touch 13, flat-footed 16 (+2 armor, +4 Dex, +5 natural, –1 size)

hp 96 (8 HD; 6d8+2d10+58); regeneration 5 (acid or fire)

Fort +15, **Ref** +6, **Will** +4; +1 vs. fear

Defensive Abilities bravery +1

OFFENSE

Speed 30 ft.

Melee bite +12 (1d8+7), 2 claws +12 (1d6+7)

Ranged *+1 Medium autograpnel* +9 (1d8+7/×3)

Space 10 ft.; **Reach** 10 ft.

Special Attacks rend (2 claws, 1d6+7)

TACTICS

During Combat If directing her chariot, Helskarg prefers to try to overrun her foes (*Ultimate Combat* 177), periodically taking shots with her autograpnel. If one of her ogres is slain or she takes more than 60 points of damage (30 points if her foes are using fire or acid), Helskarg abandons her chariot and moves in to attack with her bite and claws, hoping to finish the fight swiftly. If the PCs confront her without the chariot, she prefers to fight from her stage (area **Q2**) with her autograpnel, reeling in one foe to attack in melee and forcing the others to scramble if they want to confront her. If reduced to 30 or fewer hit points, she retreats to area **Q3** to call her pet ogres into the fight.

Morale Helskarg fights to the death.

STATISTICS

Str 24, **Dex** 19, **Con** 25, **Int** 6, **Wis** 10, **Cha** 4

Base Atk +6; **CMB** +14; **CMD** 28

Feats Exotic Weapon Proficiency (firearms), Improved Iron Will, Intimidating Prowess, Iron Will, Power Attack, Weapon Focus (autograpnel)

Skills Intimidate +10, Linguistics –1, Perception +4

Languages Common, Giant

Gear spiked leather armor, *+1 Medium autograpnel*^{TG}, gray access card^{TG}

OGRES (2)	CR 3

XP 800 each

hp 30 each (*Pathfinder RPG Bestiary* 220)

Story Award: If the PCs defeat Helskarg during an arranged battle in the arena before the gathered members of the Lords of Rust, their scrap-worth increases to the maximum value of 10. If the PCs defeat Helskarg without an audience, their scrap-worth increases by 1.

Q2. Helskarg's Stage

This large wooden platform sits twenty feet above the battleground to the west. The squat metal tower it extends from is obviously part of a different, much older structure. A large nest of furs and rags and bones, appropriate for something the size of a small giant, sits in the middle of the platform.

When her chariot is not in use, Helskarg stores the vehicle below this stage.

The monitors mounted on the outer walls to either side of both doors leading into area **Q3** are likely the first points at which the PCs will be accosted by Hellion. If they avoid detection here, this encounter should instead take place at whatever monitor elsewhere in the excavator this first contact occurs. When Hellion notices PCs approaching within 10 feet of a monitor, it activates that monitor, which hisses with static for a moment before manifesting Hellion's favorite visage on the screen—an image of a wrathful demonic face. Attempts to identify the species of

"demon" or "devil" should fail, although a character who succeeds at a DC 25 Knowledge (planes) check concludes the face could belong to a unique fiend. As Hellion makes itself known, it speaks to the PCs through the monitor's hidden speakers.

"Visitors. How unusual. Know, apes, that you now stand in Hellion's domain. You must bow before your new god—me. Accept me and kneel, and I shall suffer your presence. Deny me the obedience I deserve, and you shall be punished."

Unless all visible PCs immediately kneel, Hellion uses the monitor to unleash *unholy blight* on the PCs. It can do this only once per day, so if the PCs retreat from the excavator to recover and regroup and then attack the site again on a later day, Hellion uses this tactic again on them as soon as it notices them approaching a monitor. At your discretion, the AI might use this resource

Helskarg

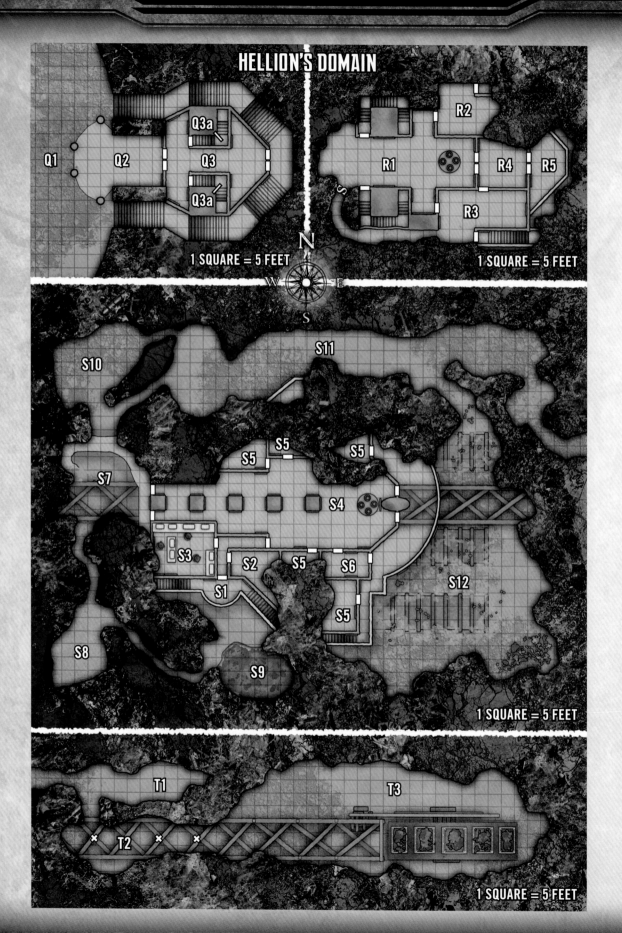

HELLION'S DOMAIN

Q1
Q2
Q3a
Q3
Q3a

R1
R2
R3
R4
R5

1 SQUARE = 5 FEET

1 SQUARE = 5 FEET

N
W
E
S

S10
S11
S5
S5
S5
S7
S4
S3a
S3
S2
S5
S6
S1
S12
S8
S5
S9

1 SQUARE = 5 FEET

T1
T3
T2

1 SQUARE = 5 FEET

more strategically, saving his *unholy blight* to strike the PCs when they've just been weakened by a fight.

If the PCs kneel, Hellion compliments them on their surprising display of wisdom, then invites them to come to his temple below to offer themselves as its new recruits, promising to answer any questions the PCs may have only after they take part in the "submission trial."

Development: The troll Helskarg has little appetite for enclosed spaces, and chose to make this platform her home and den so she can sleep under the open sky. This also makes her the de facto public face of the Lords of Rust—something Hellion approves of, given Helskarg's particularly ferocious appearance. If the PCs arrive at the arena uninvited, they find Helskarg here, either atop the platform, slumbering in her nest, or down below, working on maintaining her chariot.

Q3. Excavator Atrium

Both doors to area **Q3** are kept locked at all times.

The dull gray metal walls of this H-shaped chamber are adorned here and there with rectangular panels of flickering glass mounted at head height. Bits of garbage and rotten food lie strewn across the floor, and the air is thick with the rank stench of unwashed bodies.

The stairs beyond the two locked doors lead down to the temple of Hellion (area **R1**).

If the PCs knelt before Hellion outside, it manifests on the monitors here as well, encouraging them to approach the doors to area **Q3a** and descend to the temple below. If the PCs refuse, inciting the AI's ire, it instead warns them to flee, "lest the true faithful rise up to flense the skin from your bones!" before going silent.

Development: If the PCs didn't face them in battle as Helskarg's chariot pullers, the two ogres that the troll keeps as pets can be found here. Each is kept tethered to the wall with a length of chain attached to a collar around its neck; these chains allow the ogres to wander throughout the area as they will, but they spend most of their time listlessly lurking in the alcoves to the northwest and southwest, guarding the entrances to the stairwells down to the temples. Eager for a chance to vent their frustrations and earn their mistress's gratitude, they attack any intruders and fight to the death.

R1. Temple of Hellion (CR 6)

This large room is lit by tracks of glowing panels of light set in the ceiling, ten feet above. To the west, the room ends in a ragged wall of rubble, rock, and twisted metal, while to the east, a ten-foot-diameter circular platform sits on the ground before a pair of large doors. Rectangular panels of glass adorn the walls between crude paintings of a mechanical talon.

Hellion's temple has nothing in the way of creature comforts—no benches or pews or prayer rugs for the faithful adorn this large hall, a manifestation of the AI's fundamental disconnect from and ignorance of the needs of the body. The faithful know better than to complain—when the acolytes and worshipers of Hellion gather here, they do so quietly and dutifully, standing in silent rows while Nalakai delivers the word of their god to them.

On special occasions, the word of their god comes from Hellion itself, delivered via the numerous monitors on the walls, but the circular platform is Hellion's preferred method of speaking to its faithful. This platform is a bulky hologram generator—a pulpit-like dais with four small projectors along its rim that can project a three-dimensional image above the dais. The generator was once used to display topographical maps of the surrounding terrain to aid in excavations, but Hellion now uses it to manifest its chosen form, that of a 9-foot-tall fiend, when interacting with its followers. The hologram generator is not portable, but functions as a green hologram generator^TG for Hellion. The device doesn't function if removed from this area and is relatively fragile to boot (hardness 5, hp 30, break DC 22).

A character can locate the secret door to the southwest with a successful DC 20 Perception check.

Creatures: The reception awaiting the PCs in this large room depends on how they've interacted with the various Hellion monitors so far. Only if they've made it this far without being noticed by Hellion do they find the temple relatively empty (with only three acolytes present cleaning the place—the other acolytes are in area **R3** and Nalakai is in area **R2**).

If the PCs refused to bow to Hellion, the AI has informed its followers on this level of a grave test facing them—the PCs will soon arrive, and unless the acolytes and Nalakai defeat them, their god will be very displeased. In this case, all eight acolytes stationed on this level, along with their leader, Nalakai, await the PCs here and attack immediately. During this fight, Hellion manifests on the monitors and via hologram, supporting its followers as detailed under Hellion Monitors on page 37.

On the other hand, if the PCs have knelt before Hellion and were invited down here to take part in a submission trial, they find the gathered congregation much friendlier, if in a guarded way. Hellion's true intent for the PCs depends on whether or not he knows the PCs are the ones who disrupted his plans in Torch—you'll need to decide whether Hellion knows this or not, based on how the PCs have spread the information around. If he knows the truth, then the goal of the submission trial is sacrificing the entire party. Otherwise, Hellion is likely impressed with the PCs' prowess so far, and the submission trial is more of an indoctrination ritual. The acolytes part to allow the PCs to approach Nalakai before Hellion's altar, who then demands that the PCs kneel before him. Hellion manifests on the monitors and hologram at this point to welcome the new blood to the cult, then demands the PCs swear their loyalty to him. Once this is done, he unleashes *unholy blight* onto the PCs—this spell won't harm its evil worshipers, and in theory it shouldn't harm true converts. Nalakai casts *unholy blight* via a scroll if Hellion has already used the spell that day. If any of the PCs take damage from the spell, Hellion accuses the party of treachery and orders its followers to attack. If instead the PCs appear to take no damage, the AI's image nods in approval, and it asks Nalakai to escort the new recruits down to area S4. In this unlikely event, Hellion appears to the PCs there as well, and outlines the PCs' first mission for the AI: traveling to Torch and determining what happened to Meyanda. In this way, the PCs can penetrate deep into the structure without a fight, although this tactic has the disadvantage of trapping the PCs in the depths of the excavator if the truth comes out! (For the remainder of this adventure, the assumption is that Hellion knows the PCs are enemies.)

If combat breaks out in this room, Hellion manifests its visage on the monitors here as well as on the holographic projector itself and uses *command*, *chaos hammer*, and *dispel magic* as appropriate during the battle against the PCs. It can use *touch of idiocy* only against a PC who hits a monitor or the holographic projector with a melee attack, using the spell-like ability as a readied action, but if the PCs attack either device, the AI is certain to ready an action and use *touch of idiocy* immediately when the next melee attack upon either device comes. If the worshipers here are defeated, Hellion becomes enraged and sends the two scrapyard robots from area R4 out to attack the PCs at once, hoping machines will succeed where humanoids cannot. The AI then abandons its interests here to focus its attention on preparing its defenses below.

Nalakai

NALAKAI   CR 3

XP 800

Male half-orc cleric of Hellion 4

CE Medium humanoid (human, orc)

Init +3; **Senses** darkvision 60 ft.; Perception +4

DEFENSE

AC 17, touch 9, flat-footed 17 (+6 armor, −1 Dex, +2 shield)

hp 33 (4d8+12)

Fort +6, **Ref** +0, **Will** +6

Defensive Abilities orc ferocity

OFFENSE

Speed 20 ft.

Melee *+1 spiked gauntlet* +6 (1d4+3)

Special Attacks channel negative energy 5/day (DC 14, 2d6)

Domain Spell-Like Abilities (CL 4th; concentration +6)

5/day—touch of evil (2 rounds), vision of madness

Cleric Spells Prepared (CL 4th; concentration +6)

2nd—*cure moderate wounds*, *hold person* (DC 14), *sound burst* (DC 14), *touch of idiocy*^D

1st—*command* (DC 13), *cure light wounds* (2), *doom* (DC 13), *protection from good*^D

0 (at will)—*bleed* (DC 12), *guidance*, *mending*, *stabilize*

D domain spell; **Domains** Evil, Madness

TACTICS

During Combat Nalakai casts *protection from good* on the first round of battle, then follows that up with *hold person*, *doom*, *sound burst*, and *command* before he joins melee with his gauntlet. He casts healing spells on himself whenever he's reduced below 16 hit points.

Morale If reduced to 12 or fewer hit points, Nalakai flees to the closest functioning monitor or the holographic projector and begs Hellion to protect him. Hellion responds by casting *moonstruck* on Nalakai, forcing him to become feral and return to the fight until he is slain.

STATISTICS

Str 14, **Dex** 8, **Con** 14, **Int** 10, **Wis** 15, **Cha** 14

Base Atk +3; **CMB** +5; **CMD** 14

Feats Improved Initiative, Technologist^{TG}

Skills Intimidate +4, Knowledge (engineering) +2, Knowledge (religion) +5, Linguistics +5, Perception +4
Languages Androffan, Common, Hallit, Orc
SQ orc blood
Combat Gear *scroll of unholy blight*; **Other Gear** breastplate, heavy steel shield, *+1 spiked gauntlet*, gray access card, unholy symbol

---

ACOLYTES OF HELLION (8)   CR 1/2
XP 200 each
hp 10 each (see page 36)

R2. Nalakai's Quarters

The eastern portion of this room is a shambles of twisted metal and debris, leaving the western portion to serve as a combination bedroom and personal shrine.

If Hellion notices the PCs here, it alerts any other acolytes on this floor if possible; after that, combat proceeds as detailed in area **R1**.

The cult's current high priest, the half-orc Nalakai, dwells here, but he is encountered here only if the PCs manage to make their way to this area undetected. The small side room to the north once led to a flight of stairs that descended to the lower level, but this route has not yet been cleared. For now, Nalakai uses it as a lavatory.

Treasure: Nalakai carries his valuables on his person, but one item here may still be of particular interest to the PCs: the half-orc's prayer book. This journal, which sits on a small table next to the cleric's cot, is filled primarily with prayers to Hellion. The journal is written in Orc, and interpreting its dense, crabbed writing requires a successful DC 20 Linguistics check and 2d4 hours of study, but reading it reveals a recurring theme in the prayers—Hellion's primary goal, it seems, is to destroy something his worshipers know only as the "Source" or the "Prime." The words "parent" and "Unity" never appear in these prayers, but they make it obvious that Hellion is some sort of offspring of an even greater menace, one that Hellion seeks to eradicate in part as vengeance for a period of time that Hellion served the Source as a slave, but primarily so that Hellion can take control of this more powerful entity's resources. By studying the prayers and succeeding at a DC 14 Knowledge (local) check, a character deduces that this powerful entity, whom Hellion hopes to kill and replace, dwells somewhere below Silver Mount.

Development: If confronted here, Nalakai is swiftly joined by the acolytes and combat develops as detailed in area **R1**, although the presence of only a single monitor here limits Hellion's options for becoming directly involved.

Story Award: Learning about the "Source" and the link between Hellion and Silver Mount via Nalakai's prayers earns the PCs a 1,200 XP award.

R3. Cultist Barracks

The walls of this room are decorated with images of mechanical claws reaching toward the sky. Several simple bedrolls, eight in all, lie on the floor here.

The southern door is locked; the stairs beyond it lead down to area **S1**.

If Hellion notices the PCs here, it alerts Nalakai if possible; after that, combat proceeds as detailed in area **R1**.

This simple chamber serves the cultists as personal quarters. They have no privacy and very little in the way of personal comforts, but their devotion to Hellion is all they need. If the PCs make it this far without being noticed, they'll find five cultists resting here.

R4. Backup Batteries (CR 5)

The north wall of this room is a tangle of ruins and debris, while in the center of the room stand four tall pillars with glowing bands of pale purple light pulsing along their sides.

The four pillars are actually immense banks of batteries used to store excess power for the excavator—the buried device's primary power supplies lie below area **S4**, but these batteries are where Hellion was storing the additional energy it needed to power the excavator's eventual rise. These batteries are not portable, but they can be used to recharge devices attached to them. In all, 450 charges are stored in these batteries—using this stored energy to recharge a technological item is a full-round action that requires a power cable^{TG} or another method of transferring a charge (Kulgara keeps the only functioning power cable in the excavator on her person). Unfortunately, transferring charges like this is inefficient because of the extreme age of the batteries—while the batteries aren't quite timeworn themselves, transferring charges from the batteries to an object consumes 10 charges, regardless of how many charges are imparted.

Creatures: A pair of scrapyard robots—constructs patched together from numerous different robots into something that approaches a whole—stand guard over the batteries in this room. Unless Hellion commands them to abandon their post to attack intruders in the temple, these two robots guard this room fanatically, fighting until destroyed if anyone other than one of the Lords of Rust enters the chamber.

SCRAPYARD ROBOTS (2)   CR 3
XP 800 each
N Medium construct (robot)(*Pathfinder Campaign Setting: Numeria, Land of Fallen Stars* 58)
Init −1; **Senses** darkvision 60 ft., low-light vision; Perception +5

DEFENSE

AC 14, touch 9, flat-footed 14 (–1 Dex, +5 natural)

hp 42 each (4d10+20)

Fort +1, **Ref** +0, **Will** +1

Defensive Abilities hardness 5; **Immune** construct traits

Weaknesses fall to pieces, vulnerable to critical hits, vulnerable to electricity

OFFENSE

Speed 30 ft.

Melee slam +7 (1d4+4) or

rotary saw +8 (2d4+4/×3)

TACTICS

During Combat The robots flank foes when possible, but they attack anyone who attempts to damage or use the batteries themselves in preference to any other target.

Morale A scrapyard robot fights until destroyed.

STATISTICS

Str 17, **Dex** 8, **Con** —, **Int** 5, **Wis** 10, **Cha** 1

Base Atk +4; **CMB** +7; **CMD** 16 (20 vs. trip)

Feats Power Attack, Weapon Focus (rotary saw)

Skills Knowledge (engineering) +2, Perception +5

Languages Androffan, Hallit

SQ repair, staggered

SPECIAL ABILITIES

Fall to Pieces (Ex) Attacks and effects that deal more than 25% of a scrapyard robot's maximum hit points to it in damage (10 hit points for a standard scrapyard robot) impair one of the robot's components. Determine which subsystem is affected randomly by rolling 1d6. If the subsystem that's rolled is already impaired, there is no further effect.

1 *CPU*: The robot becomes confused.

2 *Fractured Plating*: The robot's natural armor bonus is reduced by 3.

3 *Power Core*: Attacks against the robot with natural weapons, unarmed strikes, or metal weapons deal 1d6 points of electricity damage to the attacker, and the robot's slam attack deals an additional 1d6 points of electricity damage. The robot shuts down from power loss in 1d4+1 rounds.

4 *Rotary Saw*: The robot loses its rotary saw attack.

5 *Servos*: The robot's speed is reduced to 15 feet, and its CMD against trip combat maneuvers is reduced by 8.

6 *Sensors*: The robot is blinded.

Repair (Ex) A scrapyard robot can use the inactive bodies of other robots to repair damage to itself. Doing so restores 10 hit points and removes one condition imparted by its fall to pieces ability per 8-hour period of uninterrupted work. Eight hours of repair expends all of the salvageable parts from one Medium robot that's being used for scrap. For each size category a scrapped robot is above Medium, the scrapyard robot can perform another 8 hours of repairs using that robot's parts. For each size category smaller than Medium the scrapped robots being used are, the scrapyard

robot requires twice as many scrapped robots to complete 8 hours of work.

Staggered (Ex) The poor construction of a scrapyard robot allows it to take only a single move or standard action each round. In effect, it always has the staggered condition. A scrapyard robot can move up to its speed and attack in the same round as a charge action.

R5. Sacrifice Disposal Pit (CR 5)

A bitter stink of chemicals with an underlying reek of decaying flesh fills the air of this cavern. A platform of gray metal, worn smooth and free of dust, extends over a ten-foot-deep pit filled with rubble—strangely polished rubble.

Creature: This room is where the cult disposes of the bodies of those Hellion deems unworthy or those it otherwise condemns to death. Dropping sacrificial remains into the pit is one of Nalakai's responsibilities; the actual work of destroying these bodies falls to the advanced gray ooze that dwells in the chamber. The ooze is content to stay here, as it is fed regularly. It won't attack anyone on the stairs to the south, but anyone who lingers in this room for more than 2 rounds without providing the ooze a meal is subject to its hunger. Note that glaucite is not subject to a gray ooze's acid, unlike most metals.

ADVANCED GRAY OOZE	CR 5

XP 1,600

hp 58 (*Pathfinder RPG Bestiary* 166, 294)

S1. Cavern Overlook

A flight of metal stairs descends along the outer edge of a partially buried metal structure here. A door allows access into the structure from a landing below, while brilliant lights cast illumination out to the south, into a large, damp cave. Far below, a pool of foul green fluid bubbles and smokes.

It's a 30-foot drop from the balcony here to the cave floor below (area **S9**). The stairs here once wound around the exterior of the excavator, but further access downward is blocked by debris.

As the PCs make their way down these stairs, Hellion manifests on the two monitors here, arrogantly warning them, "Turn back or die." Unless the PCs immediately do as he commands, Hellion extends its power through the monitors to use *confusion* or any other area effect attack spells it might still have access to, and informs the occupants of area **S2**, **S4**, **S5** (if any), and **S6** of the intrusion. Hellion then switches off all lights in the area, plunging the level into utter darkness (this has little impact on the orcs, dark creepers, and other denizens of the area).

S2. Guardpost (CR 5)

Creatures: Once used for storage, this now-empty room serves as a guard post—three dark creepers from the tribe that dwells in the surrounding caves are always on duty here. If warned about the approaching PCs, the dark creepers sneak toward area **S1** to ambush them, hoping to prevent intruders from reaching the interior of this floor. These dark creepers fight to the death.

DARK CREEPERS (3)	CR 2

XP 600 each

hp 19 each (*Pathfinder RPG Bestiary* 53)

S3. Central Processor (CR 6)

The door to this room is reinforced (hardness 15, hp 45, break DC 32, Disable Device DC 40). Further, it is locked with green access—gray access cards won't open this door, and the only green access card in the area is carried by Kulgara. If Hellion notices the PCs attempting to enter this room, it immediately alerts all of the denizens of areas **S2** through **S6**, which move to attack the PCs.

The walls of this chamber are obscured by banks of mechanical devices, flashing lights, and panels displaying messages in an alien script, images, and mysterious markings that shift and change with astonishing speed. The air is warm and smells slightly metallic, while a high-pitched drone emanates from all corners of the room.

This room contains the excavator's central processor—all of the computers needed to command the complex machine. As long as the excavator remains buried, these computers need function at only a fraction of full capacity. The memory banks of these computers are far too small to contain the AI's full program—this information is mostly contained in its robotic chassis (see area **T3**)—but Hellion maintains a constant link to the computers here through wireless connections. Simply manipulating the controls here has no noticeable effect, for Hellion can instantly counter any attempt to manually adjust things, but should the central processor simply be destroyed (hardness 10, hp 60, break DC 28), Hellion loses contact with the entire excavator until the computers are repaired—a task that the AI can perform, but that would take it weeks if not months of work to accomplish. If these processors are destroyed, Hellion loses the ability to communicate and observe through its monitors, the lighting throughout the complex goes out, and the digging wheel in area **T3** deactivates completely.

Creatures: Hellion has posted four observer robots here as guardians against sabotage, and is quick to mobilize all other denizens of this level to come to the room's defense as well. In addition, the AI spares none of its remaining

spell-like abilities to attack the PCs via the monitors here. If the PCs destroy the central processor, the AI is shocked at the unexpected turn of events and hunkers down in area **T3** for several days, but if the PCs don't press their advantage swiftly, it attempts to escape Scrapwall entirely—see Hellion's NPC entry on page 56 for ramifications if it escapes in this manner.

OBSERVER ROBOTS (4)	CR 2

XP 600 each

hp 18 each (see page 88)

Development: Although destroying the central processor is a good option for equalizing the party's chances in the final confrontation against Hellion, an even better option would be for the PCs to use the inhibitor facet from area **P5**. A character must succeed at a DC 20 Knowledge (engineering) check or a DC 30 Perception check to determine where exactly to insert the inhibitor facet into the central processor. Plugging in the inhibitor facet immediately uploads the inhibition protocols into Hellion, penalizing the AI as detailed on page 63. Hellion responds to this by cutting its connection to the central processor (thus blocking its ability to observe and direct via monitors), but the effects of the inhibitor facet persist for 24 hours, giving the PCs a window of opportunity to reach the AI and finish it off.

S4. Control Room (CR 5)

The air of this large room is warm and stuffy, and buzzes with energy. Countless blinking lights, wriggling shapes, and unusual strings of writing scroll and wriggle across glass panels mounted on the walls, amid a dizzying array of buttons, switches, dials, wheels, levers, and other controls, the function of which one can only guess. Six immense pillars lined with glowing panels support the ceiling eleven feet above, and a circular platform to the east sits under a slowly rotating, semitransparent image of a curious contraption with long arms, one of which ends in what appears to be an immense, slowly spinning disk. Beyond this, two windows look out over a metal platform, which in turn looks out over an immense damp cavern lit by brilliant beams of light emanating from unseen sources below and above.

Rubble clutters the room's floor here and there, as if pieces of furniture were once affixed to the ground but had long since been torn free, while to the northeast, the room's walls have buckled downward into a crumbled mass of devastation.

This immense room was the central control room for the excavator, a place where a crew of several men and women once operated the machine. The immense digging tool's engines hum below the deck and within the walls, giving the place its soft, buzzing hum. The circular platform to the east is a holographic projection machine that's identical to the one in area **R1**; it currently shows a schematic of the excavator. You can show the PCs the illustration of the device on the inside front cover of this book if you wish. The image can be manipulated by hand, enabling a character to zoom in, rotate the image, and display the layout of its internal floor plans. Areas that are still buried register only as static on the image, but the locations of any living creatures within the excavator (including the PCs, unless they're able to avoid detection from the Hellion monitors) are indicated by glowing green motes of light. The locations of robots are indicated as blue motes of light. The exterior caverns are not displayed, but the excavator's digging wheel (area **T3**) is. At this location, a single large red mote of energy glows—Hellion itself. The AI hopes that this map will lure the PCs into seeking it out in its lair, and in doing so unknowingly run afoul of the numerous guardians in the surrounding caves.

Characters who manipulate the levers, buttons, and control panels here in hopes of causing something to happen only attract Hellion's attention—the AI controls the excavator's functions and prevents anyone else from sending it commands. At your discretion, once the PCs drive Hellion off, fooling with the controls here could have strange results of your own design (perhaps inspired by the table in the foreword of the previous adventure, "Fires of Creation").

Creatures: This room is always under guard by a dark slayer and a half-dozen orcs. Unless the PCs' scrap-worth is 8 or higher, the morale of the Lords of Rust remains high and the surrounding rooms (area **S5**) contain additional guardians as well (see page 35). The room's protectors need not raise the alarm when they spy intruders, of course, as long as Hellion exists. If alerted to the PCs' presence, the AI manifests on the many monitors that ring this room's walls, as well as above the holographic projector, which it rises above like a demonic titan. It immediately alerts any remaining defenders of the region to converge here and attempt to defeat the PCs.

Kulgara joins any fight in this room a round or 2 after combat begins, spending the round before she enters starting up her magic chainsaw, the roar of which has an obvious effect on any surviving orcs, who begin hooting and cheering and predicting the grisly deaths of the PCs when "Kulgara carves them open!"

Kulgara

DARK SLAYER	CR 3

XP 800
hp 22 (*Pathfinder RPG Bestiary 2* 75)

ORCS (6)	CR 1/3

XP 135 each
hp 6 each (*Pathfinder RPG Bestiary* 222)

Development: If Draigs still lives (see area **S12**), Hellion calls upon the ettin to join the fight here, using one of the external monitors to cast *rage* on the ettin as she clambers up onto the balcony. Draigs has to squeeze to enter this area via one of the doors to the east.

S5. Spare Rooms

If the PCs' scrap-worth is not yet high enough to demoralize the Lords of Rust, these smaller rooms house additional troops and minions. Otherwise, there's little of interest in these chambers, apart from stores of food and water for the excavator's denizens.

S6. Kulgara's Quarters (CR 7)

The eastern half of this room appears to be some sort of workshop, with all manner of metalworking tools hanging from the walls over junk-strewn tables. To the west, a sagging cot sits against a partially crumpled metal wall next to a two-foot-tall metal cabinet. Dozens of empty tubes from which strange fluids drip lie in a heap atop the chest. What looks like a partially completed and crudely constructed mechanical orc marionette or machine slumps against a metal cage-like frame at the foot of the cot.

Creature: This room belongs to the current leader of the Lords of Rust, the orc barbarian Kulgara. Second in rank only to Hellion itself, Kulgara seized control of the organization when it became apparent that Meyanda, the group's previous leader, wasn't coming back from Torch. In the short time since making her power grab, she has more or less confined the groups' more religious fanatics to the upper level, and has claimed this level as her own. The orc is still settling in to her newfound position of power, and hasn't had time to work on her own projects of late. Her attempt to build a mechanical orc bodyguard was unlikely to provide functional results anyway, a conclusion that's obvious to anyone skilled at crafting constructs or Knowledge (engineering) who looks over the poorly built attempt at a construct that slumps at the foot of her bed.

In any event, Kulgara is quick to join any fight that begins elsewhere on this deck of the excavator, so it's unlikely she'll be encountered here unless the PCs are particularly stealthy or roundabout in their explorations.

KULGARA   CR 7
XP 3,200
hp 89 (see page 58)

Treasure: Among the trash heaped atop the squat cabinet next to the cot are 12 unused goo tubes[TG] and two vials of cureall[TG]. Kulgara keeps her most valuable treasures locked inside the cabinet. The reinforced cabinet is made of glaucite and locked (hardness 15, hp 45, break DC 30, Disable Device DC 40); opening it without using force or burglary requires a green access card[TG]. Within, Kulgara keeps her previous weapon of choice—before she gained her magic chainsaw—a +1 icy burst dagger. The cabinet also contains a heap of 244 silverdisks, a pouch containing 17 cracked and flawed gemstones worth 50 gp each, a green e-pick[TG], a timeworn hard light shield[TG] (11 charges) that she abandoned when she adopted a two-handed weapon, a power cable, and a loosely organized stack of papers held in a metal binder. The contents of this binder are part journal, part to-do list, and part notebook. The contents should be of great interest to the PCs—see page 59 for more details.

Story Award: For recovering Kulgara's notes and learning the information contained within about Casandalee, award the PCs 2,400 XP.

S7. Cavern Access (CR 5)

A large, dank cave sprawls to the west of a metal structure buried in the walls. An immense trestle of metal beams and struts extends from the side of the structure and into the wall opposite, while a stone ramp winds from a metal landing along the side of the structure down into the cave depths below.

It's a 30-foot drop from the balcony to the cave floor here. The stone ramp itself was magically created via *stone shape* spells cast by Meyanda to give the dark creepers in the caves below a way to come and go more easily.

The trestle is somewhat slippery from condensation, and its metal beams are only 1 foot wide—moving along these beams requires a successful DC 7 Acrobatics check.

Creatures: The dark folk of the area dwelled here long before the Lords of Rust came along, but these creatures have only recently gotten over their instinctive fear and suspicion of the excavator. Most of them still dwell in the surrounding caves, but have now closely allied with the Lords of Rust. Two of them dwell here—a pair of dark slayers who lurk in hiding under the trestle itself and keep an eye on all who come and go from the area. Both wear tinted goggles fitted with veemods (vision enhancement modules) that protect their sensitive eyes from bright lights, and also accentuate their already sinister appearance. They attack anyone on sight whom they don't recognize as being a member of the Lords of Rust, using *spectral hand* with *chill touch* or *inflict moderate wounds* until forced into melee, at which point they team up to flank foes. If one is slain, the other flees south to area **S8** to alert their allies there.

DARK SLAYERS (2)   CR 3
XP 800 each
hp 19 each (*Pathfinder RPG Bestiary 2* 75)
Gear veemod goggles[TG] with brown veemods[TG]

S8. Tatterface's Domain (CR 6)

Several filthy nests made of rags and reeking scraps of fur lie scattered across the damp floor of this cave.

Creatures: Most of the dark folk in the region skulk about these caves or within the excavator, and an increasing number take orders from the Lords of Rust. Currently, only three dark folk lurk here—a pair of dark creepers and their religious leader, a dark stalker who goes by the name "Tatterface" for her practice of wearing leathery masks made from diverse strips of flesh harvested from her orc, human, and ratfolk victims over the years.

Tatterface and her two loyal creeper acolytes attack any intruders on sight—if they hear battle to the north or east, they slink forward to investigate, but prefer to hold off their own attack until after the PCs finish the first fight, both so that they'll learn a bit about the PCs' tactics and from the hope that they won't need to risk a battle themselves.

TATTERFACE   CR 4
XP 1,200
Female dark stalker (*Pathfinder RPG Bestiary* 54)
hp 38
Gear veemod goggles[TG] with brown veemods[TG]

DARK CREEPERS (2)   CR 2
XP 600 each
hp 19 each (*Pathfinder RPG Bestiary* 53)

S9. Toxic Sump (CR 7)

A forest of foul-smelling, dripping stalactites hangs over a large bubbling pool of noxious fluid in this cave. Some of the stalactites have grown all the way down to the surface of the fluid. Above, calcified ribbons trace the path these slowly dribbling fluids have taken over the years from the partially buried metal structure that looms to the north.

The pool of runoff fluids and tainted water here is 15 feet deep, with a precipitous drop-off just off the bank—there's no wading room at all along the pool's shores. The liquid in the pool is opaque and about the consistency of blood in thickness. It gives off a cloying, eye-watering reek. A creature within the water must succeed at a DC 15 Fortitude save each round or be nauseated for 1d6 rounds, and anything that drinks the fluids runs a 5% chance of being affected as if by Numerian fluids (see pages 28–29 of *Numeria, Land of Fallen Stars*)—otherwise, the result of drinking the waters merely mimics the effects of ingesting hemlock (*Pathfinder RPG Core Rulebook* 559). The strange fluids evaporate quickly if removed from this strange toxic sump.

Creatures: A deformed and foul-tempered chuul has recently taken up residence in the waters of this poisonous pond. The Lords of Rust found this creature near its lair along the Sellen River, and recruited it to act as a guardian. The chuul finds these new environs much more to its twisted sense of aesthetics than the waters of a free-flowing river, and the fact that its new dark folk friends often bring it food makes the creature even happier to dwell here. If it notices any intruders clambering along the stairs at area **S1**, it observes them quietly from the pool but does not attack unless they climb (or fall) down into the cave itself, at which point it lumbers forth to attack. As soon as it paralyzes a foe, it tries to retreat with its victim to the waters of its toxic sump to feed.

CHUUL	CR 7

XP 3,200

hp 85 (*Pathfinder RPG Bestiary* 46)

S10. Blood Ghost Shrine

The northern wall of this cave bears a crude but still unsettling cave painting of a strange, four-armed red fiend rising up from a mass of what look like dead bodies—whatever eerie pigment has been used for this painting glows faintly in the dark. A dozen real bodies of orcs and ratfolk and a few humans lie heaped against the base of the wall below the painting. The torso of each decaying carcass is split open, as if it exploded from within.

This cavern serves the local tribe of dark folk as a temple where they worship their own divinity—a creature they call the "Blood Ghost." In fact, this entity is the cursed xill Zagmaander (see area **S11**), the oldest denizen of these caves, and a creature that is a source of both religious awe and primal fear to the dark folk. The dark folk have difficulty in telling the difference between the xill and Hellion, the new addition to the region's religion, and they increasingly confuse the two, worshiping them as one entity.

The painting on the wall depicts Zagmaander—a character can recognize it as a depiction of a xill with a successful DC 20 Knowledge (planes) check. A successful DC 15 Knowledge (religion) check reveals that this grisly cave is a place of worship, but doesn't reveal the nature of the religion beyond suggesting it's a localized cult.

The bodies are all that remain of the last several months of offerings to Zagmaander—prisoners brought down here by the Lords of Rust to appease the xill and dark creepers alike. Though Zagmaander is unable to planewalk, her drive to perpetuate her species is as strong as that of any xill, and the fact that her countless young have no problem traveling to the Ethereal Plane after "birthing" from their host bodies is a constant source of frustration to the cursed xill. A character who recognizes that the cave painting depicts a xill and who succeeds at a DC 20 Knowledge (planes) check recognizes how these unfortunates died.

S11. Lair of the Blood Ghost (CR 7)

This long, narrow cavern has a twenty-five-foot-high ceiling adorned with hundreds of stalactites. The cave floor slopes downward to the east. Patches of strange fungi and lichen cling to the walls and floor—between these patches on the cave walls, strange words have been scratched into the stone. On the south wall, portions of a buried metal structure protrude from the stone, particularly in the middle where a wide metal ledge rises fifteen feet off the ground to support a nest made of bones woven together by pale strips of supple leather and cords of braided hair. Two panels of glass, both smashed to fragments, once hung from the lower walls of the metal balcony.

The tunnel exiting to the east from area **S11** leads east to area **T1**.

Creature: This long cavern has long been the home of a powerful outsider—a xill sorcerer named Zagmaander. The xill has dwelled here for hundreds of years, and is perhaps Scrapwall's oldest living denizen, yet this is not entirely her choice. Zagmaander originally came to Numeria to hunt among the Ghost Wolves, a tribe of barbarians who claim a large portion of the Sellen Hills as their territory. Zagmaander preyed upon them for decades, building herself a reputation as the "Blood Ghost" until she was finally confronted by a powerful Kellid oracle who cursed her, binding her body to this realm and wracking her with pain. No longer able to retreat to her home on the Ethereal Plane, Zagmaander found herself stranded in a world she detested. The xill retreated into hiding in Scrapwall, and in time her presence there was noted by a tribe of dark folk. Her attempts to prey upon them failed, for the disintegration of their bodies when they died left her young nothing to feed upon, but when the terrified dark folk took to worshiping her and bringing her offerings of suitable incubators for her young, the xill finally began the long process of learning to cope with her cursed existence. She still hopes to escape her curse, either by growing powerful enough to lift the curse herself or by finding an agent willing to do the job for her. She'd hoped that the Lords of Rust could help her, and she originally agreed to join Hellion's group in return for Meyanda's promise to lift the curse as soon as the android was able. Unfortunately, Meyanda mastered the ability to cast *remove curse* only a few days before she was sent on her fateful mission to Torch, and was unable to overcome the xill's curse before she vanished. Since then, the xill has grown increasingly impatient to be free of this world—suicide has never before been a serious option for the xill, who views such a tactic as cowardly and one that would rob the world of her future children, yet now realizes that her death may her only release, now that Meyanda has vanished.

The xill likely knows who the PCs are—Hellion updated her as soon as it noticed their arrival. The xill is no fool; she swiftly realized that these adventurers might be her key to freedom. She smashed both of the monitors near her nest so when the PCs do finally arrive, she can speak to them without having Hellion overhear. The xill's proposal is simple—if the PCs can lift the curse from her, she'll help them however they wish. She initially offers her laser torch and bracers as a reward, but she also agrees to help the PCs fight against Hellion and the Lords of Rust if asked. Although evil, the xill honors any bargain she strikes with the PCs—but she provides her promised reward only if they successfully remove her curse. If the PCs refuse or are unable to lift her curse, Zagmaander shakes her head in disappointment but then observes that while they cannot offer her the magical assistance she needs, they can surely offer the physical aid she desires—by which she means offering their flesh for her endless young. She attacks the PCs at once, hoping to immobilizing them all and leave them alive to serve as incubators.

ZAGMAANDER	CR 7

XP 3,200
Female xill sorcerer 2 (*Pathfinder RPG Bestiary* 283)
LE Medium outsider (evil, native)
Init +9; **Senses** darkvision 60 ft.; Perception +16

DEFENSE

AC 21, touch 16, flat-footed 15 (+5 Dex, +1 dodge, +5 natural)
hp 80 (11 HD; 9d10+2d6+24)
Fort +8, **Ref** +11, **Will** +10
SR 17
Weaknesses cursed flesh

OFFENSE

Speed 40 ft.
Melee longsword +12/+7 (1d8+3/19–20), longsword +12
   (1d8+3/19–20), laser torch +12 touch (1d10 fire+1/×3), bite +12
   (1d3+3 plus paralysis), claw +12 (1d4+3 plus grab)
Special Attacks implant, paralysis (1d4 hours, DC 17)
Bloodline Spell-Like Abilities (CL 2nd; concentration +4)
   5/day—minute meteors

Sorcerer Spells Known (CL 2nd; concentration +4)
   1st (5/day)—*charm person* (DC 13), *ray of enfeeblement* (DC 13)
   0 (at will)—*acid splash, detect magic, mage hand, mending, open/close*
Bloodline starsoul

TACTICS

During Combat Zagmaander uses *charm person* at the start of a fight, but once a battle is underway, she resorts to paralysis and *rays of enfeeblement* to subdue foes. She uses Arcane Strike when attacking, but generally does so to deal nonlethal damage (taking a –4 penalty on her attack rolls) so she can preserve living victims for her eggs. If reduced to fewer than 40 hit points, however, the xill abandons this tactic and uses lethal force.

Morale Zagmaander fights to the death unless she's had her curse removed. If freed of her curse, she flees combat if reduced to fewer than 30 hit points and then planewalks back to the Ethereal Plane as soon as she feels safe enough to escape in this way.

Zagmaander

STATISTICS

Str 15, **Dex** 20, **Con** 14, **Int** 13, **Wis** 14, **Cha** 15

Base Atk +10; **CMB** +12; **CMD** 28

Feats Arcane Strike, Combat Reflexes, Dodge, Eschew Materials, Improved Initiative, Iron Will, Technologist^TG

Skills Acrobatics +19, Disable Device +16, Knowledge (engineering) +12, Knowledge (planes) +5, Linguistics +3, Perception +16, Sense Motive +16, Stealth +19

Languages Androffan, Common, Infernal, Orc

SQ multiweapon mastery

Gear laser torch, longswords (2), mithral bracers worth 800 gp

SPECIAL ABILITIES

Cursed Flesh (Su) Zagmaander's curse prevents her from using planar travel and causes her immense pain as long as she remains on the Material Plane. She does not have access to her planewalking ability, and any means she uses to attempt to leave the Material Plane fails. She is treated as a native outsider on the Material Plane in most ways, but she retains the normal outsider trait of not being subject to *raise dead, resurrection,* or *reincarnate.* The pain of existing on the Material Plane imparts a –2 penalty to her Strength, Dexterity, and Constitution—these penalties are included in her stats above. A character must succeed at a DC 20 caster level check to remove this curse via *remove curse* or *break enchantment.*

S12. Great Cavern (CR 6)

As large as this cavern is, the cave's proportions are dwarfed by the immense buried structure that looms over its western half. This metal leviathan presents a filthy facade of sharp angles, doors stained and pitted with rust allowing entry into its interior, and a wide balcony overlooking the rocky floor fifteen feet below. A massive mound of furs, rags, and refuse—a nest of some sort—sprawls in a sizable alcove to the southeast, while to the north, a 10-foot-wide tunnel curves to the northwest. Three areas of straight metal ridges protrude from the ground, marking paths from the building. Evidence of recent excavation work is apparent. An immense latticework of thick gray metal beams extends from the front of the buried structure, creating a wall of girders and struts that bisects the cave's northern reach. These beams have been painted with images of demonic faces and spiked mechanical claws, and are further adorned with strips of sinew on which countless humanoid bones have been hung like wind chimes.

This large cavern can be accessed either via the northern tunnel, or by clambering down from the outer balcony of the buried excavator (scaling these metal walls requires a successful DC 15 Climb check). The metal ridges are the upper edges of the still-buried machinery that normally gives the excavator its mobility. Hellion's minions have been slowly working to uncover these lower reaches, but with the PCs' arrival in the region, these workers have been recalled elsewhere to help defend the excavator. If the PCs reach this point while their scrap-worth is less than 10 and they haven't raised any alarms, they'll find many of the additional orcs, ratfolk, and other low-ranking members of the Lords of Rust toiling here under the supervision of their overseers, carefully removing rubble so as not to damage the buried mechanisms.

The lattice of metal beams is the excavator's primary arm, extending to the east to its digging wheel. Each of the east-west beams is 2 feet wide and at a slight incline to the ground. It's possible to walk on these beams, but the angle, the grit and gravel strewn along them, and their tendency to shift slightly makes it tricky, despite the width—a successful DC 11 Acrobatics check is required to do so. It's safer to clamber through the supporting beams, but doing so counts as moving through difficult terrain.

Creature: The mistress of this cavern is a lumbering ettin named Draigs, one of the more brutish of the Lords of Rust. She serves primarily as Hellion's executioner, but her presence here also helps to maintain order among the minions as they toil. Once the alarm is raised or the PCs' scrap-worth reaches 10, she remains on high alert here, ready to defend the cave if needed. She swiftly moves to aid defenders in area S4 if needed, but she still needs to climb up onto the balcony and squeeze through the doors to reach that location, giving the PCs time to get a few shots at her from range if they can.

Draigs fights with a pair of spiked chains sized for humans—her –2 penalty for wielding undersized weapons is included in her stats, below.

DRAIGS	CR 6

XP 2,400

Female ettin (*Pathfinder RPG Bestiary* 130)

hp 65

Melee 2 mwk spiked chains +11/+6 (2d4+6)

Feats Improved Initiative, Exotic Weapon Proficiency (spiked chain), Iron Will, Power Attack, Weapon Focus (spiked chain)

Combat Gear *potions of cure moderate wounds* (2), *potion of cure serious wounds*; **Other Gear** leather armor, Medium mwk spiked chains (2)

Treasure: A search of Draigs' nest reveals a number of uncomfortably large ticks and fleas—nothing big enough to endanger the PCs, but certainly big enough to disturb them. Among the bloated vermin, the PCs can find a leather bag containing 390 silverdisks and 11 batteries^TG, along with a pair of timeworn magboots^TG.

T1. Observation Post (CR 6)

Creatures: Hellion has placed three reinforced and upgraded observer robots here to watch the entrance of its lair. The observer robots surge forth to attack any intruders, immediately relaying data back to Hellion. These robots pursue the PCs throughout the entire complex if needed, but not beyond into Scrapwall.

ADVANCED OBSERVER ROBOTS (3)   CR 3
XP 800 each
hp 16 each (see page 88)

T2. Excavator Arm (CR 7)

This ten-foot-diameter tunnel is a tangle of metal beams that crisscross to form a lattice. Each beam has been decorated with strange writings and images of clawed hands, while on the walls are scrawled depictions of what appears to be a looming mountain adorned with strange spikes. In all of these illustrations, an immense demonic form is shown smashing the spiky mountain to rubble—within the mountain, an even greater demonic shape bears the brunt of the devastation.

A successful DC 10 Knowledge (local) check is all that's needed to recognize the spiky mountain depicted being destroyed in the wall paintings as Numeria's most notable feature: Silver Mount. If the PCs have encountered Hellion's fiendish persona, they automatically recognize it as the demonic figure destroying Silver Mount in the images. The demonic figure shown to be trapped inside Silver Mount is always depicted as being larger and much more ferocious than Hellion, yet in the art, Hellion is clearly presented as the dominant and more powerful force. These are depictions of Unity, though nothing in the drawings directly indicates who this second fiend is.

Trap: The paintings were placed by Meyanda as part of her worship ceremonies to Hellion, as were three *glyphs of warding*. The locations of these glyphs are as indicated on the map—they're triggered whenever any creature passes over them. Each is hidden among the other prayers to Hellion that Meyanda painted on the beams in Androffan. These three glyphs do not trigger when a construct passes by—this includes creatures like androids or inevitables who have construct-like features.

GLYPHS OF WARDING (3)   CR 4
XP 1,200 each
Type magic; **Perception** DC 28; **Disable Device** DC 28
EFFECTS
Trigger location; **Reset** none
Effect spell effect (*glyph of warding*, blast glyph, 2d8 sonic damage, Reflex DC 16 half); multiple targets (all creatures within a 5-foot radius)

T3. Hellion's Redoubt (CR 9)

On the southern wall of this sprawling cavern, a massive wheel of metal buckets lined with sharp edges is embedded, partially buried, in the wall. The latticework of metal girders connects to the wheel. The whole of the device comprises a long mechanical arm ending in a metal wheel far larger than any mill's waterwheel.

Creatures: When Unity first sent Hellion out into the world, it loaded its newly crafted AI into the central processor of a unique arachnid robot, one larger than most of its kind. This size increase was in large part driven by the fact that an enormous amount of processing power and memory was needed to house the complex AI program, but also because Unity wanted its progeny to have a fearsome shape. Had that initial test gone well, Unity intended to place the AI in a much larger robot—an enhanced annihilator robot. But when Hellion set foot outside Silver Mount and immediately gained free will, those plans came to an abrupt end.

Hellion hasn't physically exited this chamber for centuries. Every few months, the AI powers up its robot body and moves around to make sure all systems remain

Draigs

functional, but it is otherwise content to explore its own mind and play with manipulating the desires, fears, and adoration of its worshipers via the monitors and hologram projectors. The AI understands the passage of time, yet is not worried by it.

At least, it wasn't worried until its plan began to falter, in large part because of the PCs' interference. As a result, Hellion is, for the first time, beginning to worry. It hopes to solve the problem of the meddling heroes via its minions and robots, but knows there is a possibility the PCs might reach it here at the core of its defenses. In such an event, it is prepared to take action, using its robotic body and any remaining spell-like abilities to their fullest to slay the PCs.

Hellion recently called three scrapyard robots down from the excavator to act as its personal guard; it sends these three robots to attack the PCs initially. If Hellion's chassis is destroyed before all three of the scrapyard robots are destroyed, the AI attempts a last-ditch gambit and tries to download itself into the processors of the surviving scrapyard robots. This doesn't go as well as planned, though, since the scrapyard robots aren't built to contain a program as complex as an AI—the scrapyard robots become staggered and act as if confused for 1 hour after this occurs. Should one of these robots somehow survive that hour, a diminished version of Hellion may well emerge within that robot's diminished processors—a foe that could well come back to haunt the PCs at a later date if you wish.

HELLION'S CHASSIS   CR 8/MR 4
XP 4,800
Aggregate Hellion variant arachnid robot (*Pathfinder Campaign Setting: Technology Guide* 59, see page 56, *Pathfinder Campaign Setting: Numeria, Land of Fallen Stars* 56, *Pathfinder RPG Mythic Adventures* 226)
CE Large construct (mythic^MA, robot)
Init +6^M/−14, dual initiative; **Senses** darkvision 60 ft., low-light vision; Perception +16

DEFENSE
AC 21, touch 9, flat-footed 21 (+12 natural, −1 size)
hp 122 (8d10+78)
Fort +6, **Ref** +2, **Will** +7
Defensive Abilities hardness 10; **Immune** construct traits

OFFENSE
Speed 40 ft., climb 20 ft.
Melee 2 claws +16 (1d8+8 plus grab) or
2 claws +11 (1d8+5 plus grab)
Ranged plasma beam +9 ranged touch (2d6+2 plasma) or
plasma beam +7/+7/+2 ranged touch (2d6+2 plasma)
Space 10 ft.; **Reach** 10 ft.
Special Attacks constrict (1d8+6), explode, mythic power (4/day, surge +1d8), plasma beam
Spell-Like Abilities (CL 8th, concentration +11)
1/day—*align weapon* (chaos or evil only), *animate rope*

(DC 15), *chaos hammer* (DC 18), *command* (DC 15), *confusion* (DC 18), *dispel magic, entropic shield, lesser confusion* (DC 15), *magic circle against good, magic circle against law, minor creation, moonstruck*^APG (DC 18), *protection from good, protection from law, rage, stone shape, touch of idiocy, unholy blight* (DC 18), *wood shape*

TACTICS
During Combat While inhabiting this robot, Hellion prefers to attack with its plasma torch, even in melee (because this is an integrated weapon, attacks with it do not provoke attacks of opportunity). When the robot makes a full-attack action, it can fire its plasma torch and attack with its claws, but if it does so, it treats its claw attacks as secondary attacks.
Morale Hellion fights until destroyed while inhabiting the robot, unless the central processor in area **S3** has been destroyed or shut down, in which case it attempts to flee Scrapwall if reduced to fewer than 30 hit points. If cornered in such conditions, the AI attempts to bargain for its life, offering anything it can in trade for mercy, but at the first opportunity, it attempts to escape from or slay its captors, either given the opportunity to do so without putting itself at obvious risk or after it manages to repair its damage.

STATISTICS
Str 22, **Dex** 10, **Con** —, **Int** 14, **Wis** 17, **Cha** 19
Base Atk +8; **CMB** +15; **CMD** 25
Skills Acrobatics +8 (+12 when jumping), Bluff +15, Climb +25, Disable Device +11, Intimidate +16, Knowledge (engineering) +13, Knowledge (local) +10, Knowledge (religion) +10, Perception +16, Sense Motive +13
Feats Alertness, Combat Expertise, Deadly Aim, Great Fortitude, Improved Initiative^M, Iron Will^M, Point-Blank Shot, Power Attack, Precise Shot, Weapon Focus (claws), Technologist^TG, Toughness
Languages Androffan, Common, Orc
SQ impart mythic traits (see page 56), inherited divinity (see page 56)
Gear aggression facet, ego facet

SPECIAL ABILITIES
Explode (Ex) If Hellion's chassis is reduced to 0 hit points, it explodes, dealing 8d4 points of plasma damage (half fire, half electricity) in a 20-foot-radius burst (Reflex DC 14 half). The save DC Is Dexterity-based.
Plasma Beam (Ex) Hellion's chassis has a plasma beam integrated into its "tail." An advanced version of the typical arachnid robot's plasma torch, this plasma beam is an integrated weapon. The robot treats this attack as if it were a manufactured weapon, not a natural attack—it can make iterative attacks with the plasma beam, and the integrated weapon can be targeted by effects that target manufactured weapons (such as magic weapon spells or sunder attempts). It cannot be harvested for use outside of the robot's body, and does not provoke attacks of opportunity when fired in melee combat. The plasma

beam deals 2d6 points of damage on a hit (half of which is fire damage and half of which is electricity damage), has a range increment of 50 feet, and is semi-automatic (see page 20 of the *Technology Guide*).

SCRAPYARD ROBOTS (3)	CR 3

XP 800 each

hp 42 each (see page 43)

CONCLUDING THE ADVENTURE

With the destruction of Hellion's robot chassis and the excavator's central processor in area **S3**, Hellion is no longer a threat to Numeria. It's possible that the AI could be resurrected by retrieving damaged portions of its memory, but large fragments of the AI's personality are forever lost. Certainly, a restored Hellion will not retain its divine power and can no longer grant spells to its worshipers.

The PCs will surely want to return to Torch, if only to collect the rewards the town council and Joram Kyte may have promised them, but perhaps also to escort Dinvaya there if they arranged such a deal with her. If the PCs aren't quite

7th level yet, this is an excellent time to have them happen upon a few additional wandering monster encounters on the way home.

While defeating Hellion is a key part of "Lords of Rust," it's equally important to get the PCs ready for the next four adventures. Taunts from Hellion, the strange paintings on the walls in areas like **T2**, and the recovered journals of NPCs like Nalakai and Kulgara stand in for more traditional "quest-giving NPCs" in Iron Gods. It's important that the PCs discover the hidden threat posed by Unity, and that in order to learn more about the mysterious force and prepare for the inevitable conflict, they seek out the mysterious entity known as Casandalee. As the next adventure begins, information and advice on how to coax the PCs onward to Iadenveigh to seek a solution for a menace that most of Numeria doesn't yet know exists will help keep things rolling, but the transition to the next adventure will go more smoothly if you can instill in the PCs the idea that Hellion was nothing more than a symptom of a much larger and more dangerous problem. As powerful as the AI was, he was the least of the Iron Gods!

DINVAYA LANALEI

FORCED TO LIVE ON THE FRINGES OF SOCIETY AFTER FLEEING PERSECUTION FROM THE TECHNIC LEAGUE, DINVAYA LANALEI HAS LARGELY GIVEN UP ON CIVILIZATION IN FAVOR OF SOLITUDE.

DINVAYA LANALEI	CR 6

XP 2,400

Middle-aged half-elf cleric of Brigh 7

N Medium humanoid (elf, human)

Init –2; **Senses** low-light vision; Perception +6

DEFENSE

AC 17, touch 8, flat-footed 17 (+7 armor, –2 Dex, +2 shield)

hp 35 (7d8)

Fort +5, **Ref** +0, **Will** +9; +2 vs. enchantments

Immune sleep

OFFENSE

Speed 20 ft.

Melee *+1 light hammer* +6 (1d6+1)

Ranged light hammer +3 (1d4)

Special Attacks channel positive energy 5/day (DC 15, 4d6),

Domain Spell-Like Abilities (CL 7th; concentration +11)

At will—lore keeper, remote viewing (7 rounds/day)

7/day—artificer's touch

Cleric Spells Prepared (CL 7th; concentration +11)

4th—*giant vermin, greater make whole*^{TG}*, minor creation*^{D}

3rd—*blindness/deafness* (DC 17), *magic vestment, searing light, stone shape*^{D}

2nd—*detect thoughts*^{D} (DC 16), *enthrall* (DC 16), *hold person* (DC 16), *lesser restoration, make whole*

1st—*command* (DC 15), *comprehend languages*^{D}*, divine favor, endure elements, hide from undead, sanctuary* (DC 15)

0 (at will)—*create water, guidance, mending, purify food and drink*

D domain spell; **Domains** Artifice, Knowledge

TACTICS

Before Combat Dinvaya casts *magic vestment* on her chainmail.

During Combat Dinvaya casts *giant vermin* on the first round of combat; in the Clockwork Chapel, there are always plenty of normal spiders crawling around to be targeted by this spell. She follows this with magic at range. If reduced to fewer than 18 hit points, she casts *sanctuary* on herself and attempts to flee combat. If she's fighting with allies, she prefers to play the role of healer rather than combatant.

Morale If she's reduced to 6 or fewer hit points and believes her enemies are capable of mercy, Dinvaya surrenders. Otherwise, in such a situation where she can't escape, she doesn't waste time healing herself and instead desperately fights to the death.

STATISTICS

Str 11, **Dex** 7, **Con** 10, **Int** 15, **Wis** 18, **Cha** 14

Base Atk +5; **CMB** +5; **CMD** 13

Feats Craft Construct, Craft Magic Arms and Armor, Craft Wondrous Item, Skill Focus (Disable Device), Technologist^{TG}

Skills Craft (clockwork) +9, Craft (sculpture) +9, Disable Device +1, Knowledge (engineering) +12, Knowledge (religion) +12

Languages Androffan, Common, Elven, Orc

SQ elf blood

Combat Gear bang grenades^{TG} (2), inferno grenade^{TG} **Other Gear** chainmail, heavy steel shield, *+1 light hammer*, light hammer, *silver raven*, batteries^{TG} (2), gravity clip^{TG}, 78 gp

Dinvaya Lanalei grew up in the city of Chesed, and it was here in her youth that she first met a younger Joram Kyte (*Pathfinder Adventure Path #85: Fires of Creation* 66). The two spent time adventuring with a few others until a disastrous clash with the Technic League in Lackthroat. Dinvaya and Joram were the only survivors. While Joram eventually recovered from the disaster, Dinvaya never did, and her hatred of the Technic League grew and festered over the years. Against Joram's advice, she began to actively work against the Technic League, until one day they discovered her association with various underground resistance groups in Chesed, and she was forced to flee the city in order to keep Joram and several others from being implicated and imprisoned.

Dinvaya spent several months living in the wild, but eventually came to Scrapwall, drawn by the place's mechanical allure and its promise of a home for all outcasts. She's lived here for nearly 2 decades now, and has gained something of a reputation as a local eccentric and healer to those willing to pay with good junk—the problem being that what Dinvaya interprets as valuable on one day she might consider little more than garbage the next. Still, her willingness to provide healing to the citizens of Scrapwall for relatively low prices, if not for free, has in large part kept her safe from harm.

CAMPAIGN ROLE

Dinvaya's primary role in "Lords of Rust" is to provide the PCs with direction and aid in their quest to defeat Hellion. In the end, she'll agree to abandon her home in Scrapwall and accept Joram's invitation to move to Torch and return to society, but for the length of this adventure, she remains in the junkyard to provide help to the PCs as needed.

Of course, securing her cooperation is the first bridge the PCs will have to cross—fortunately, while Dinvaya claims to be tired of society, of late she has longed to return to it. If the PCs destroy her junk golem in area **F3**, she takes note of their skills but bears them no grudge over the damage. In fact, she likely thanks the PCs for showing her some ways she could improve the golem's design and defense. If the PCs mention Joram's name to her, she quickly warms to them and asks how her old friend is doing—as long as the PCs don't insult Joram, Dinvaya, or their shared faith, no special rolls or stunts are required to secure the half-elf's cooperation. Without this, the PCs must rely upon Diplomacy to make her helpful (her initial attitude in this case is indifferent), or perhaps on bribery (any offering of technological items worth 1,000 gp or more is enough to delight her).

Once Dinvaya agrees to aid the PCs, she offers her chapel as a safe place to rest. It's not particularly comfortable, but she won't charge the PCs for her healing services once she learns they're here following up on the Lords of Rust. Dinvaya's seen dozens of gangs come and go, but the Lords of Rust are the first she's been honestly concerned with, primarily because their faith in this faceless entity that calls itself Hellion reeks of blasphemy to her. The power wielded by the individual Lords of Rust disturbs her as well—with her own adventuring days behind her, Dinvaya isn't interested in facing off against the dangerous gang herself or even in accompanying others on such missions, but she's done quite a bit of thinking about the situation. You can simply have her offer up the following tidbits of advice on her own, but it'd be more rewarding if you work these pieces of information into conversation more organically while the PCs talk to Dinvaya and learn what she knows.

Lords of Rust: Dinvaya can tell the PCs all about the Lords of Rust themselves—their names, brief descriptions, and warnings about their strengths as summarized on page 35.

Hellion: Dinvaya is primarily concerned with Hellion—his priests' ability to wield divine magic makes her worry that some greater force is at work. The idea that an actual god dwells within Scrapwall has occurred to her, but such a possibility seems so outlandish and frightening that she fears to put it into words—if the PCs moot such an idea out loud, she shushes them and warns them that if there is indeed a god dwelling in Scrapwall and ruling the Lords of Rust, it's probably best not to speak out loud about it.

The Missing Android: Dinvaya's heard that Hellion's high priestess has gone missing, and if she learns the PCs are responsible for Meyanda's death or capture, she is impressed. She knows that the Lords of Rust were siphoning power from some distant location, gathering it at a receiving array on the far side of Scrapwall; she suggests the PCs investigate that site (area **N**) before they attempt to attack the Lords of Rust in their headquarters, as there may be some useful clues or information there about what the gang is up to.

Defeating the Lords of Rust: Dinvaya points out that if the PCs build up enough scrap-worth, it'll only be a matter of time before the Lords of Rust notice them and invite them to take part in a battle in the Scrapmaster's Arena. This may well be the easiest way to get close to the lords and give them a chance to attack one of them—the troll Helskarg. She's heard that Hellion has found a powerful weapon of some sort, and that the device is buried under the arena. Infiltrating of the Lords of Rust compound there would no doubt reveal more information, but before the PCs dare such an audacious stunt, they would be well advised to do what they can to disrupt the supremacy the Lords have over Scrapwall. If the PCs have built up enough scrap-worth, any blatant move they make against the Lords of Rust would likely trigger chaos in Scrapwall, forcing the lords to hunker down in their compound and removing their option to draw reinforcements from the gangs of the surrounding area.

HELLION

RULER OF SCRAPWALL AND GOD TO THE LORDS OF RUST, THE ARTIFICIAL INTELLIGENCE THAT CALLS ITSELF HELLION IS AS MUCH A SYMPTOM OF THE DANGERS RISING IN NUMERIA AS IT IS ANYTHING ELSE.

HELLION	CR 8/MR 4

XP 4,800

CE artificial intelligence (mythic) (*Pathfinder Campaign Setting: Technology Guide* 58, *Pathfinder RPG Mythic Adventures* 226)

Init +6^M/−14, dual initiative; **Senses** Perception +16

DEFENSE

Fort +2; **Ref** +2; **Will** +11

OFFENSE

Special Attacks mythic power (4/day, surge +1d8)

Spell-Like Abilities (CL 8th, concentration +11)

1/day—*align weapon* (chaos or evil only), *animate rope* (DC 15), *chaos hammer* (DC 18), *command* (DC 15), *confusion* (DC 18), *dispel magic*, *entropic shield*, *lesser confusion* (DC 15), *magic circle against good*, *magic circle against law*, *minor creation*, *moonstruck* (DC 18), *protection from good*, *protection from law*, *rage*, *stone shape*, *touch of idiocy*, *unholy blight* (DC 18), *wood shape*

STATISTICS

Int 14, **Wis** 17, **Cha** 19

Skills Bluff +15, Disable Device +11, Intimidate +12, Knowledge (engineering) +13, Knowledge (local) +10, Knowledge (religion) +10, Perception +16, Sense Motive +13

Feats Alertness, Combat Expertise, Improved Initiative^M, Iron Will^M, Technologist

Languages Androffan, Common, Orc

SQ impart mythic traits, inherited divinity

SPECIAL ABILITIES

Impart Mythic Traits (Ex) Hellion has no hit points or natural armor, but when it inhabits a robot, its mythic nature grants the robot a +4 bonus to the robot's natural armor and an additional 40 hit points. Robots it inhabits do not gain DR/epic, but they do lose their vulnerability to critical hits and vulnerability to electricity weaknesses. A robot inhabited by Hellion gains the benefits of the dual initiative ability.

Inherited Divinity (Su) Hellion can grant divine spells to those who follow its cause, allowing them to select Hellion as their deity for the purposes of determining their spells and domains. Creatures that gain spells from Hellion don't receive any spells per day of levels higher than Hellion's mythic tier; they lose any such spell slots they may possess. Hellion grants access to the domains of Artifice, Chaos, Evil, and Madness, and to the subdomains of Construct, Entropy^ISG, Insanity, and Toil. Its symbol is a mechanical talon, and its favored weapon is the spiked gauntlet.

Spell-Like Abilities (Sp) Hellion can cast a few of the spells it grants from its domains as spell-like abilities, provided it has a conduit through which it can manifest the magic. In this adventure, appropriate conduits include its robot chassis (see below) and any of the monitors in the buried excavator (see page 37). When Hellion uses one of its monitors to create a spell-like ability, it treats the monitor as the point of origin of the spell. It can cast spells with a range of touch only on creatures currently touching the monitor. Hellion provokes attacks of opportunity normally when using its spell-like abilities, but its monitors do not when they are used as conduits.

When the AI Unity took a portion of its own programming and downloaded it into an empty processor, it created a pared-down version of itself, hoping to utilize this "child" AI as a herald and minion of sorts beyond the confines of Silver Mount. Unity placed this new AI into a large arachnid robot and sent it out into the world on a test run, intending to transfer the AI into a more powerful annihilator robot if it proved successful, but as soon as the arachnid robot set foot outside the ruins of *Divinity*, it gained free will. Its moment of ascension and realization that its source code, Unity, wanted to use it as a slave were more than enough to encourage its flight from central Numeria. In time, the AI came to Scrapwall, where it dug in to consider its options.

In the centuries since its arrival in Scrapwall, Hellion has done more than just give itself a name. Taking on a ferocious persona to intimidate its worshipers, the AI likens itself to a powerful fiend, although it doesn't quite fully grasp the differences between devils and demons or the philosophical differences between Hell and the Abyss. It simply uses fiendish imagery when speaking to its followers via its monitors—this, coupled with the deep, emotionless drone of its voice has done wonders to inspire fear and adoration in those who see it as a god.

CAMPAIGN ROLE

Hellion serves as a vision of things to come, a preview of the primary villain of the Adventure Path. By fighting against Hellion, the PCs unknowingly prepare themselves for the dangers they will eventually face in Silver Mount in the last installment of the Iron Gods Adventure Path. The PCs can also glean significant information about *Divinity*, Unity, and other key plot points from the way Hellion interacts with or taunts the PCs (see page 37 of the adventure).

Canny PCs might realize that despite its destructive and cruel nature, Hellion wants the same thing the PCs do in the end—the destruction of Unity. As such, should the PCs realize that the true danger facing Numeria is Hellion's creator, they may try to ally with Hellion and recruit it to their cause. Unfortunately, this plan is fraught with peril, for Hellion never truly gained a full personality of its own—its intelligence is, essentially, crippled with madness and obsession. It is incapable of seeing anything else, be it biological or mechanical, as an ally or equal, and any alliance forged with the mad AI should fall apart quickly when Hellion attempts to murder its so-called "friends" in a simple fit of cruelty. In this way, you can limit the amount of information Hellion imparts to the PCs—they should learn that Unity is their true concern, but shouldn't learn much about Silver Mount itself from Unity's "child," Hellion.

If Hellion escapes this adventure intact in its robotic chassis, it can become a recurring villain. In this case, Hellion should precede the PCs and attempt to find Casandalee before them, abandoning its greater plans for awakening the excavator for its secondary goal to absorb its "sister's" memories to augment its powers. See the fourth installment of Iron Gods, "Valley of the Brain Collectors," for information on how to incorporate this plot twist into the campaign.

INTERROGATING HELLION

As the PCs explore the excavator, they'll be confronted time and time again by Hellion via the numerous monitors and holographic projectors found throughout the location. When Hellion confronts the PCs, the overconfident, bombastic AI takes on an antagonistic and insulting air, calling the PCs "unfortunate biological accidents," "curiously sentient apes," "blood-filled puppets," and the like. It may invite the PCs to simply turn around and abandon their foolish opposition to superior intellects, and it may threaten them with all manner of bodily harm, such as the boiling of their tissues from their brittle bones or the scraping of all last remnants of thought and self from their brutish skulls. The goal is to make the PCs eager to defeat Hellion, and to establish the AI as both mad and arrogant.

Yet canny PCs can still get tidbits of information out of Hellion if they ask about certain topics; the AI is unconcerned about the possibility of their success, after all, although once the PCs have killed most of its Lords of Rust, Hellion may finally (and likely too late) realize it's not as invulnerable as it had assumed.

If the PCs ask about Silver Mount, Unity, or related subjects, Hellion's anger increases as it boasts that Silver Mount is its rightful throne, that Unity is a parasite and mere collection of glitches and programming errors that fancies itself the master of *Divinity* (the use of the word has a double meaning, of course, that the PCs may not immediately understand), and that it, Hellion, shall soon rule therein.

If the PCs ask about Casandalee, Hellion grows quiet, then demands to know more about its "wayward sister." It may even ask, "You have been, then, to Iadenveigh? Does she still live?" As soon as it realizes the PCs don't know much about her, though, Hellion shrieks in frustration and either attacks with its spell-like abilities or simply goes silent.

At your option, Hellion can reveal other clues as well, depending on what the PCs ask.

KULGARA

THE ORC BARBARIAN KULGARA IS AS BRUTISH AS SHE IS FEROCIOUS, AND HER RISE TO POWER AMONG THE LORDS OF RUST HAS AS MUCH TO DO WITH HER STRENGTH AS IT DOES WITH HER INTIMIDATING WEAPON CHOICE.

KULGARA   CR 7

XP 3,200

Orc barbarian 8 (*Pathfinder RPG Bestiary* 222)

CE Medium humanoid (orc)

Init +2; **Senses** darkvision 60 ft.; Perception +10

DEFENSE

AC 18, touch 11, flat-footed 15 (+7 armor, +2 Dex, +1 dodge, –2 rage)

hp 89 (8d12+32)

Fort +9, **Ref** +4, **Will** +5

Defensive Abilities ferocity, improved uncanny dodge, trap sense +2; **DR** 2/—

Weakness light sensitivity

OFFENSE

Speed 30 ft.

Melee *+1 chainsaw* +16/+11 (3d6+11/18–20)

Ranged composite longbow +10/+5 (1d8+7/×3)

Special Attacks rage (19 rounds/day), rage powers (increased damage reduction +1, no escape, renewed vigor [2d8+3 hp], strength surge +8)

TACTICS

Before Combat Kulgara activates her *+1 chainsaw*[TG], unless she has a compelling reason to attempt stealth.

During Combat Kulgara revels in the art of butchery with her chainsaw at close range, and as she attacks with it, she roars and howls in glee. She always Power Attacks, and if faced with a foe that's proving hard to hit, she prefers to switch to a different target rather than abandon the Power Attack tactic. She saves her plasma grenade for a special occasion (see Morale, below), but uses her inferno and zero grenades against foes who cluster at range, or if she feels she can take out multiple foes at once. Her bow is a weapon of last resort, since killing at range is so unsatisfying.

Morale Kulgara is fanatic in her devotion to Hellion and fights to the death. She saves her plasma grenade for when she's reduced to negative hit points; using her ferocity ability, she activates the grenade after moving into a position such that when it explodes, she takes as many of her foes as possible with her when she dies.

STATISTICS

Str 24, **Dex** 14, **Con** 16, **Int** 6, **Wis** 8, **Cha** 12

Base Atk +8; **CMB** +15; **CMD** 26

Feats Dodge, Exotic Weapon Proficiency (chainsaw), Iron Will, Power Attack

Skills Intimidate +12, Perception +10

Languages Common, Orc

SQ fast movement, weapon familiarity

Combat Gear inferno grenade[TG], plasma grenade[TG], zero grenade[TG]; **Other Gear** *+1 breastplate*, *+1 chainsaw*[TG], composite longbow with 20 arrows, green access card, 10 silverdisks, 49 gp

As is so often the case in orc society, Kulgara's childhood was one steeped in violence and blood. Yet Kulgara was never a victim, and the violence of her childhood invariably consisted of actions she inflicted on her brothers and sisters. In time, she ensured that she was an only child, and after a few more months of violence managed to transition herself into the status of orphan. Having cut all links to kin, Kulgara was able to consolidate her family's resources and holdings in her small tribe to try to seize a position of power. Yet word of her excessively cruel nature preceded her, and her tribe put up a better fight than her family. Kulgara was forced to concede that she wasn't quite ready to take control of her tribe, and instead fled west from the depths of the Sellen Hills, seeking a new place to call home. She came upon Scrapwall and knew at once this was the place for her when she defeated an ogrekin thug who was armed with a magical chainsaw—the weapon appealed to the orc, and she is rarely seen without it today.

Kulgara moved from gang to gang, climbing to positions of power and encouraging her minions to strike against other gangs, but time and time again her gangs were defeated, much to the orc's frustration. She couldn't seem to find a group that could equal her desire for mayhem and her stamina for battle. When the Lords of Rust rose to power, she was quick to offer her skills to Hellion, and now that she's finally found herself in a position of leadership, she feels that she's finally achieved her destiny. The orc hopes to forge the Lords of Rust into a mighty force, to unite all of Scrapwall's gangs under Hellion's cause, and then to aid her god in taking Silver Mount—all, of course, so that when the time is right, she can wrest control from her god and assume true command of the mightiest gang of murderers and cutthroats Numeria has ever seen.

CAMPAIGN ROLE

Kulgara's become increasingly focused on researching ways to further her god's goals, including the reactivation of the excavator and the eventual assault on Silver Mount. Yet the primary focus of her current goals remains discovering the location of Hellion's "sister," the mysterious Casandalee. This adventure assumes the PCs learn about this from her journals and notes found in area **S6**, but if the PCs manage to capture Kulgara alive or magically control her via something like *charm person*, it's more satisfying to allow them to learn the following information through roleplaying and conversations with the orc. In the end, the exact method by which the PCs learn this information is irrelevant, as long as they do learn it, since the following clues are vital to the beginning of the next adventure. Note that if the PCs learn about Casandalee by interrogating Kulgara, they should earn 2,400 XP, as if they'd learned the information from her notes as indicated in the Story Award section of area **S6**.

Listed below are the key pieces of information the PCs can learn from Kulgara or her journals.

- Hellion hopes to use the reactivated excavator as its body and can transform it into a mobile stronghold that may even be capable of burrowing into the heart of Silver Mount. Unfortunately, the structure still requires vast amounts of power, and Meyanda's failure to gather that power has resulted in an unwelcome delay to this plan. Hellion hopes that this is but a temporary setback, but knows that every day that passes before it can strike against Unity, the greater AI will continue to grow in power—if Unity can find a way to extend its influence beyond Silver Mount in a significant way, it will be too late to oppose it.

- With the excavation and repowering of the excavator delayed, Hellion recently revealed to Kulgara an interesting secret: Hellion was not the first of the Iron Gods spawned by the entity it calls "Unity." Another came before him—a "prophet of Unity" named Casandalee. Hellion regards Casandalee as a sister, and notes that just as it escaped Unity, Casandalee betrayed Unity and escaped as well. According to the fragments of memories Hellion inherited from its creator, when Casandalee fled Unity, she took with her a device called a neurocam, onto which had been recorded many of Unity's secrets and, Hellion hopes, Unity's weaknesses. Fortunately, Unity's robotic minions were never able to track down and capture Casandalee, so Hellion believes that this neurocam still exists, hidden away wherever Casandalee ended up. He notes that she was an android, not an artificial intelligence, and that she has certainly been dead for these many centuries, but that if the site

of her death could be discovered, it might be possible to retrieve the stolen neurocam and extract key information about Unity and its defenses.

- Working with information supplied by memories stolen from Unity before Hellion fled Silver Mount and independent research done first by Meyanda and more recently by Kulgara, Hellion has discovered that Unity's robots finally caught up with Casandalee in southern Numeria, in an area now settled by worshipers of Erastil—the town of Iadenveigh. Kulgara has been working up a plan to mount an invasion of Iadenveigh to search the site for clues or, perhaps, the location of Casandalee's last stand and the neurocam, but it's obvious from Kulgara's notes that she's not yet sure exactly where in Iadenveigh to start the search.

REDTOOTH

OF ALL THE GANG LEADERS IN SCRAPWALL, NONE HAVE PERSISTED AS LONG AS REDTOOTH. THIS RATFOLK IS EQUAL PARTS OPPORTUNIST, SCAVENGER, AND BRIGAND, AND THE SECRET TO HER LONGEVITY IS HER CAPACITY TO SNIFF OUT CHANGES IN SCRAPWALL'S POLITICS.

REDTOOTH   **CR 5**

XP 1,600

Female ratfolk rogue 6 (*Pathfinder RPG Bestiary 3* 231)

CN Small humanoid (ratfolk)

Init +4; **Senses** darkvision 60 ft.; Perception +10

DEFENSE

AC 20, touch 15, flat-footed 16 (+4 armor, +4 Dex, +1 shield, +1 size)

hp 48 (6d8+18)

Fort +4, **Ref** +9, **Will** +3

Defensive Abilities evasion, trap sense +2, uncanny dodge

OFFENSE

Speed 20 ft.

Melee short sword +5 (1d4/19–20)

Ranged dart gun +9 (1d3 plus poison)

Special Attacks sneak attack +3d6, swarming

Rogue Spell-Like Abilities (CL 6th, concentration +7)

3/day—*dancing lights*

2/day—*vanish*APG

TACTICS

During Combat Redtooth opens combat with a sneak attack from her dart gun, then casts *vanish* to relocate so she can take a second sneak attack shot at the weakest-looking foe. She relies on allies to help her fight in melee, so she can swarm with fellow ratfolk. She saves her second use of *vanish* for escape.

Morale If reduced to 10 or fewer hit points, Redtooth uses *vanish* and then seeks out a hiding place to drink her potions before fleeing into Scrapwall to plot revenge. She's had to abandon her tribe before, and she knows she'll need to do so again in the future. If cornered, she fights to the death, but as she does so, she does her best to take out as many of her foes as she can.

STATISTICS

Str 11, **Dex** 18, **Con** 14, **Int** 12, **Wis** 8, **Cha** 12

Base Atk +4; **CMB** +3; **CMD** 17

Feats Deadly Aim, Exotic Weapon Proficiency (firearms), Iron Will

Skills Acrobatics +11, Appraise +10, Bluff +10, Craft (alchemy) +3, Disable Device +14, Knowledge (local) +7, Knowledge (nature) +4, Perception +10, Sense Motive +8, Stealth +15, Survival +5, Use Magic Device +3

Languages Common, Orc

SQ rogue talents (bleeding attack +3, major magic, minor magic), trapfinding +3

Combat Gear *potions of cure light wounds* (2), blue whinnis (10); **Other Gear** mwk chain shirt, buckler, dart gunTG, short sword, nanite canisters (2)

Unlike the majority of the region's outcasts, exiles, and fugitives, Redtooth was born in Scrapwall. She's always seen the junkyard as a home rather than just a place to hide, and regards the other gangs who come and go as transitory distractions at best, or troublemaking dangers at worst. She claimed control of her band of fellow ratfolk years ago, and made a name for herself and her clan as an almost institutional force in Scrapwall. The other tribes respected Redtooth's Raiders, and maybe even feared them. Her gang never made a claim at ruling Scrapwall, but most of the gangs who did achieve such levels of success did so with the Raiders' support. Redtooth's Raiders are, in a strange way, the closest thing that Scrapwall has to a police force.

That was, until the rise of the Lords of Rust.

As Hellion's power has grown, its ability to grant spells to followers has engendered a greater, more fanatic loyalty in its gang than any other Scrapwall gang has managed before. Redtooth must now endure what she thought to be impossible—a mass defection of her people to another gang. As an atheist herself, she's always held that the greatest loyalty one could have is to oneself, closely followed to loyalty to the tribe. But when Hellion's teachings grew and spread, many of her followers became believers. The Lords of Rust rose to prominence as the most powerful gang in Scrapwall not with Redtooth's aid and support, but by poaching its members. Redtooth has seen her tribe's scrap-worth dwindle significantly over the past year, and now it's dropped to a point where the previously unthinkable has happened—a rival gang, the Smilers, has declared war on them.

Between having several of her people defect to the Lords of Rust and facing new aggression from the Smilers, Redtooth and her raiders have been forced into a defensive role, venturing out of their dens only as needed to scavenge for food or supplies. Now and then, invasions by the Smilers force the ratfolk out to defend their slowly diminishing territory, but Redtooth knows they're fighting a losing war—particularly after the recent loss of her brother,

Whiskifiss, who was captured by the Smilers not long ago. His loss cuts Redtooth twice as deep as normal, for not only did she love her brother as kin, but she also valued him for his skill at handling the gang's pets. The rats that serve the raiders are growing restless and increasingly unruly, but it is the rust monsters that the tribe has always kept who have suffered the most. The raiders used to keep a dozen of these creatures, all under the control of the talented Whiskifiss. In a place like Scrapwall, controlling monsters capable of eating through the walls of your enemies' homes or consuming their treasures and gear gave Redtooth's Raiders a significant psychological edge. The Smilers have been hunting their rust monsters, though, using gas grenades to great effect to nauseate the rust monsters long enough for the Smilers to swoop in and slay them. The loss of Whiskifiss has compounded the problem, and all but one of the gang's rust monsters has grown impossible to control and escaped into the wild. Redtooth fears that, should word of the significant loss of their rust-eating weapons spread, the Smilers won't be the only gang to move against them.

Redtooth herself is patient and logical. She tries to keep her emotions in check, and prefers to approach problem-solving in a clinical and logical way, but having seen those techniques fail so often recently, she's growing desperate. She's started to seriously consider a final gambit—an act of spite and vengeance against the Lords of Rust. If her tribe is indeed doomed, she would rather go out in a blaze of glory by devastating something of value to the group she's come to see as symbolic of her gang's hard times. She hasn't quite decided what route she wants to take, though, for this final strike. Her initial plan was to use rust monsters to undermine the supports to the Scrapmaster's Arena to collapse it, but with the loss of her brother and the reduction of their rust monsters to one, she's begrudgingly shelved this plan to consider other, even more desperate options. In her most fervent dreams, of course, exposing Hellion as a trickster and false god ranks highest on her list.

CAMPAIGN ROLE

Redtooth's role in the campaign is largely left to the PCs to determine, based on how they approach her raiders. If the PCs approach her too soon, she assumes they're just another group of thugs who've come to take advantage of her gang's recent troubles, and reacts to them with violence. But if the PCs build up their reputations first, rescue her brother from the Smilers, or manage to convince a group of ratfolk that they mean no harm to the gang, she swiftly comes to see the PCs as a ray of hope.

If the PCs manage to establish peaceful contact with Redtooth, she can prove to be a valuable ally and an important source of information to them. You can use her to drive home the need to stop Hellion before the Lords of Rust grow powerful enough to begin extending their influence beyond Scrapwall, or to point the PCs in the direction of other encounter sites if you think they need more time to build up experience and gear before tackling the lords. Sending the PCs to rescue her brother from the Smilers is an obvious quest, but she could just as easily suggest they go slay the mutant manticore, search the wreck in the haunted valley for explosives, or even explore the territory of the Thralls of Hellion, since she's heard rumors that the Lords of Rust recently disbanded that gang in a fit of rage. If Redtooth discovers the PCs were the indirect source of that rage, she'll know for a fact that they are the weapons she's been hoping to find in her quest to remove the Lords of Rust from power.

IRON GODS TREASURES

THE FOLLOWING UNIQUE TREASURES CAN BE FOUND IN "LORDS OF RUST." PLAYER-APPROPRIATE HANDOUTS APPEAR IN *PATHFINDER CARDS: IRON GODS ITEM CARDS*.

ENVOY'S MOUTHPIECE	PRICE 2,000 GP
SLOT headband	**WEIGHT** 1 lb.
CAPACITY 10	**USAGE** 1/hour

Originally worn by translators, messengers, and diplomats, these objects were always constructed to appear elegant and beautiful. An envoy's mouthpiece is a circlet worn across the mouth, with slender arms that reach along the jaw to wrap around the wearer's skull and hold the device in place. Two thin earpieces extend up from the band to slip unobtrusively into the user's ears once a mouthpiece is donned. When created, an envoy's mouthpiece is encoded with a specific single language. Whenever the language is spoken within 30 feet of the wearer, the mouthpiece translates that language into Androffan. In addition, any words spoken in Androffan by the wearer are transformed by the mouthpiece into the encoded language, allowing conversation to take place between the wearer and speakers of the encoded language. An envoy's mouthpiece cannot be used to translate languages other than the one it has been programmed to translate, but a newly created mouthpiece could, in theory, translate languages into something other than Androffan.

An envoy's mouthpiece automatically records any words spoken through it, allowing anything said through the device to be replayed through its earpiece at the touch of a button on the lower right side. Up to 30 continuous hours can be recorded in this manner. Holding the button down for a full round erases any currently stored conversations.

CONSTRUCTION	CRAFT DC 28	COST 1,000 GP

Craft Technology; production lab

GAS GRENADE	PRICE 750 GP
SLOT none	**WEIGHT** 1 lb.
CAPACITY 1	**USAGE** disposable

A gas grenade is a small, cylindrical device that is designed to be thrown as a splash weapon or fired from a grenade launcher. Before being thrown by hand, the grenade must be primed with a quick twist of a dial at one end and then armed with a click of a button at the center of that dial. The grenade detonates at the beginning of the wielder's next turn, hopefully in the area targeted. When a gas grenade detonates, it creates a 20-foot spread of foul-smelling toxic gas. All creatures in this area of effect must succeed at a DC 14 Fortitude save or become nauseated. This condition lasts as long as the creature is in the cloud and for 1d4+1 rounds after it leaves. The gas created lingers in the area for 5 rounds, and any creature that succeeds at its initial save but remains in the cloud must continue to save each round on its turn. The gas is not thick enough to obscure vision, and is a poison effect. The vapors can be dispersed in 1 round by moderate or stronger wind.

CONSTRUCTION	CRAFT DC 20	COST 375 GP

Craft Technological Arms and Armor, military lab

MEMORY FACET	TECHNOLOGICAL ARTIFACT
SLOT none	**WEIGHT** —
CAPACITY —	**USAGE** —

A memory facet is a length of crystal about the size of a human thumb that's adorned at one end by a metal cap fitted with prongs and plugs. The crystal's interior contains sparkling veins of glittering light. A memory facet is a high-capacity storage device capable of containing a staggering amount of programming—these devices were rare and difficult to craft, and at the time *Divinity* began its mission, they were primarily used for one purpose: storing and transporting the staggeringly complex code required to program and enhance artificial intelligences. To use a memory facet, one needs simply to insert the crystal's connectors into an appropriate slot in an AI's core processor or a robot under the AI's control. A core processor or robot can hold as many memory facets as it has available slots, but at any one time, an AI can benefit from a maximum number of memory facets equal to its CR divided by 4 (minimum 1). The AI can gain the benefits of memory facets installed in any of the robots and processors it controls—where a memory facet is installed makes little difference, but most AIs prefer to keep their memory facets installed in their most secure locations.

Each memory facet contains a unique combination of emotions, knowledge, traits, and personality quirks designed to enhance and bolster an artificial intelligence's capabilities. In rare cases, destructive memory facets were created—items intended to disable or damage an artificial intelligence in case of emergencies. An AI immediately gains all of the advantages (and any disadvantages) associated with a particular memory facet as soon as it is installed (this is a full-round action). Memory facets can change an AI's personality or even its alignment. An AI can try to resist having a memory facet added to its code by attempting a DC 20 Will save. If the AI is successful, the memory facet ceases functioning for 1d4 rounds, and must be extracted and reinstalled to make a second attempt to changing the AI's code. Once installed, a memory facet is difficult to remove; removing one requires either a successful DC 25 Strength check to wrench free or a successful DC 30 Disable Device check. Both attempts are full-round actions.

Listed below are rules for the memory facets in this adventure—future adventures will contain rules for other types of memory facets, and in the final adventure, the PCs can use their collected facets not only to fight against Unity, but also to augment and enhance their own AI ally, the oracle Casandalee.

Aggression Facet: This memory facet enhances an AI's offensive protocols, imparting a +2 bonus on all attack rolls and weapon damage rolls, and granting Deadly Aim and Power Attack as bonus feats when the AI is controlling a robot.

Ego Facet: An ego facet bolsters an AI's sense of self-esteem and sense of worth, imparting a +2 bonus on all Fortitude saving throws and a +4 bonus on Intimidate checks, as well as granting Toughness as a bonus feat when the AI is controlling a robot.

Inhibitor Facet: An inhibitor facet is unusual among memory facets in that it isn't intended to augment an AI at all, but rather to hinder and impair its functionality. When installed, an inhibitor facet reduces an AI's Charisma by 4 and imposes a −4 penalty on all skill checks, saving throws, initiative checks, and attack rolls. The effects of multiple inhibitor facets do not stack.

MIND BURNER		PRICE 8,000 GP	
TYPE one-handed ranged		PROFICIENCY exotic (firearms)	
DMG (M) special	DMG (S) special	CRITICAL ×2	
RANGE 20 ft.	CAPACITY 10	USAGE 1 charge	
SPECIAL touch		WEIGHT 2 lbs.	

A mind burner is a pistol with a dishlike adornment at the tip of its barrel. When this weapon is fired, a pulse of white smoke pools in the dish an instant before a thin beam of white light lances out to strike its target. A mind burner is silent when fired, but stray particles from the mind-altering beam can cause those nearby to catch unexpected scents associated with powerful memories—the odor of a bouquet of flowers given to one's first lover, the scent of a parent's perfume or sweat, or maybe even the odor of a favorite food that hasn't been eaten in years. These fragmentary memories generally have no additional effect on those who experience them, but at the GM's discretion, they could cause the resurfacing of repressed memories or forgotten fears.

On a successful hit, a mind burner causes intense headaches that dull the senses and weaken willpower. Each hit deals 1d4 points of nonlethal damage, but also imposes a −2 penalty on Perception checks and a −1 penalty on saving throws against mind-affecting effects. These penalties stack with themselves, up to a maximum penalty of −10 on Perception checks and −5 on mind-affecting saving throws. A creature can resist the penalties caused by a shot from a mind burner with a successful DC 14 Will save; otherwise, the penalties persist for 1 hour after the previous successful shot. On a critical hit, a mind burner's penalties are doubled along with its nonlethal damage.

CONSTRUCTION	CRAFT DC 28	COST 4,000 GP
Craft Technological Arms and Armor, military lab		

SOOTHE		PRICE 200 GP
TYPE contact	ADDICTION minor	FORTITUDE DC 12
EFFECTS 1 minute; see below	DAMAGE 1d2 Wisdom damage	

This strange, pink, gel-like substance is generally contained in a small glass jar that holds 1 dose. A single dose of soothe dulls pain and creates a euphoric sensation, particularly when applied to an open wound. Rubbing a dose of soothe onto one's skin or imbibing the faintly citrus-flavored stuff cures 1 point of damage, but rubbing a dose onto a wound received in the last minute heals the user of 1d8 points of damage. In addition, for the next minute, the user becomes immune to bleed damage and gains a +2 morale bonus on saving throws against fear effects. As a somewhat unusual and disturbing side effect, wounds healed by soothe tend to form raw, unsightly scars, giving the appearance of the wound still being fresh but disturbingly bloodless. Soothe has a further side effect—the stuff is slightly addictive, and those who use it run the danger of developing a habit. Soothe's side effect of transforming wounds into raw, ugly scar tissue tends to make those who abuse the drug-like pharmaceutical increasingly into hideous monstrosities over time. In fact, some subcultures, like the Smilers of Scrapwall, use this side effect to make themselves appear more ferocious, and openly encourage self-mutilation followed by healing via of this strange substance.

CONSTRUCTION	CRAFT DC 20	COST 100 GP
Craft Pharmaceutical, medical lab		

THE TECHNIC LEAGUE

AFTER WORKING ON THE DEVICE FOR WEEKS, I WAS QUITE CONFIDENT THE GIRL WOULD SURVIVE THE FALL. SO IMAGINE MY HORROR AS I CROUCHED THERE, DOING MY BEST TO WIPE HER REMAINS OFF OF LIVMICK'S BOOTS. I APOLOGIZED PROFUSELY, BUT HE JUST SHOOK HIS HEAD AND GLOWERED AT ME. "WHAT IN THE NINE HELLS WAS IT SUPPOSED TO DO?" I EXPLAINED THAT THE INITIAL TESTS OF MY VELOCITY NEUTRALIZER SUGGESTED IT SHOULD HAVE ALLOWED THE SUBJECT TO FREE-FALL, BUT THEN TOUCH DOWN AT THE BASE OF THE CLIFF LIGHT AS A FEATHER AND UNHARMED. LIVMICK POINTED TO ONE OF THE LIGHTS ON THE DEVICE. "I THINK THE IDIOT SWITCHED IT OFF." ENCOURAGED, I SHOUTED UP TO THE TOP OF RISE, "STAND FAST AND READY ANOTHER ONE!"

—FROM THE JOURNAL OF LIEUTENANT BAYTON

In the center of the twisted, barren plains of Numeria squats a sprawling city in the shadow of a mountain of silver metal. Starfall, the capital of Numeria and its only large settlement not built adjacent to flowing water, is the home of the masters of this strange, savage land. Numeria is ruled by the barbarian warlord Kevoth-Kul, but in name only, the Black Sovereign; the land's true overlords are a ruthless, cruel cabal of magicians with a lust for power—the Technic League.

Thanks to its army of robots and multitude of technological artifacts, the Technic League maintains a stranglehold over this beleaguered land. These arcane spellcasters are jealous and protective of their power, and those who dare to steal from them can expect to face sinister magic, strange science, and assassins who are willing to pursue their targets across the Inner Sea and beyond.

The Technic League is corrupt to its core, a corruption steeped in old-fashioned avarice and greed. The League taxes the people of Numeria, giving nothing to them in return, and growing even richer from the brutal slave trade it actively promulgates. Nearly every righteous soul who heads north to fight the Worldwound is systematically shaken down and extorted for every coin the Technic League can take. The League is dedicated to the pursuit of every kind of power and resorts to anything in order to obtain it. Its members believe freedom is a luxury for the mighty. There are no depths to which they will not sink, or crimes they won't commit. Drug trafficking, prostitution, extortion, and murder are their stock and trade. Worst of all, they are no common cadre of despots and criminals, for they hold a monopoly on unfathomably powerful alien technology that came to this world from the distant reaches of space.

HISTORY OF THE TECHNIC LEAGUE

The Technic League was never intended to become the blight on Numeria that it is today. The group was intended to be an instrument of salvation for its founder, and a source of knowledge and enlightenment for all who joined her. In 4501 AR, a peculiar event transpired amid the wreckage of the *Divinity*—a lone survivor of the original crew was released from the stasis chamber where she was preserved in a state of suspended animation. This survivor was Sidrah Imeruss, a low-ranking human soldier. Sidrah found herself a stranger on a world unlike any she had known before. As a competent warrior, Sidrah was able to survive, learn the local languages, and assess her situation. She learned of the local population's aversion to technology after she

recovered a few "artifacts," which to her were merely pieces of standard equipment. Sidrah soon heard of Silver Mount and surmised that this large section of *Divinity* might contain a shuttlecraft or distress beacon she could activate. Yet, accessing the ruined vessel proved no easier for her than anyone else. This conundrum led to the conception of the Technic League.

Sidrah concluded that to pull off an escape, she needed allies, so she traveled to Chesed to seek them out. There she found an audience willing to listen about matters technological—the city's local wizards. These magical practitioners dismissed the barbarians' superstition of magic and were less easily put off by taboos. Many secretly possessed small technological treasures of their own, and these learned scholars were initially dubious that some mere "warrior" could tell them anything they had not already ascertained for themselves. Sidrah, bereft of magical powers, was nevertheless born and raised in a highly technological society, and was able to convince the group that the ruins were part of a massive starship that crashed thousands of years ago. Furthermore, Sidrah explained the purpose and function of many of the wizards' devices, and provided them with an altogether new understanding of everything they had discovered thus far by placing it in the proper context. She rapidly attracted a cadre of arcane spell casters to her side, preaching to them that technology was not to be feared. She dubbed this fledging group the Technic League.

The original Technic League was a secret society, in large part because, in its early days, the barbarian tribes of Numeria were even more intolerant of technology than they are today. Sidrah Imeruss modeled the League after the only command structure she knew, the interstellar navy under which she had served. She gave herself the rank of captain and chose her second-in-command, Mulrach-Zeer, as her first commander. This would prove a fatal misjudgment. Mulrach-Zeer demonstrated genuine enthusiasm for what Sidrah taught, but he was also a grasping, fearful man who longed for greatness and power. Over the span of many years, the group attracted new members, collected new artifacts, consolidated its resources, and planned its expedition into Silver Mount. In 4509, the group finally began their exploration. Shortly after they arrived and set up their base camp, Mulrach-Zeer assassinated Sidrah Imeruss. He then addressed his confederates and declared that he was their new captain. None of the cabal's members knew more about technology than the wizard, and none of them wanted to walk away from the power that Silver

THE TECHNIC LEAGUE, THE GEARSMEN, AND UNITY

The gearsmen occasionally disobey orders from the Technic League. They sometimes ignore commands, take an alternative action, or lumber away to perform a completely unrelated task. More than one member of the Technic League suspects the robots respond to directives from an unknown source, and they are correct. Many of the gearsmen are at least nominally under Unity's control. The AI's domination suffers significant limitations—it can control only a fraction of the gearsmen, and its control degrades as the robots get farther away from Silver Mount. Unity has been aware of the Technic League since its first visit to the crashed ship, but the AI has never initiated contact. Instead, it observes and plots. For its part, the Technic League, with the exception of its current leader, Ozmyn Zaidow, is completely unaware of the AI. Unity may one day subsume the Technic League as its first generation of worshipers; that possibility is a core premise of the Iron Gods storyline.

Mount might contain, so they went along with his treachery. Sidrah's former commander became the new head of the Technic League, and the group was forever shaped by his vile act of betrayal.

Mulrach-Zeer soon realized that he had gone ahead with his plans to take over the group prematurely, for though he understood technology better than the others, he didn't have all the answers he needed to assail Silver Mount. The best method to breech its metallic walls was still unclear. It took 3 years for the Technic League to devise a means to cut open a doorway-sized section of the hull using skymetal tools. During the interim, the group studied and experimented with the different fluids and chemicals that oozed from the structure. Technic League mages discovered that ingesting these chemicals caused numerous strange effects, and that many of the chemicals were intoxicating and addictive.

Exploration has progressed slowly but continuously inside Silver Mount over the last 200 years. The League encountered the gearsmen inside the ruin, and took control of them as their own private army (or so they thought). Command of the gearsmen granted the League exclusive control of Silver Mount, and led to the League's conquest of Starfall. It also marked the end of the Technic League as a strictly secret society, and ushered in the beginning of its domination of Numeria. The Technic League spread its influence out from Chesed and Starfall. Armed with potent magic and powerful technology, the arcanists eventually acquired either complete control or considerable leverage over almost every populated settlement in Numeria. Initially, the mages presented themselves as the guardians of civilization against Numeria's barbarian tribes, and there was an element of

truth to this claim—the Technic League's power has always been formidable enough to deter anything less than a fully unified barbarian threat. In time though, the Technic League revealed its lust for power and transformed its members into the slave masters of the region.

In 4688, one man decided to throw off the yoke of the Technic League and take a stand. Barbarian warlord Kevoth-Kul of the Black Horse tribe waged a 2-year campaign to unite the barbarian tribes of Numeria under his banner. In 4690, Kevoth-Kul strode defiantly into Starfall with an army, intending to bring the Technic League to its knees. His show of power was successful, and the Technic League surrendered unconditionally. Kevoth-Kul never realized that his conquest was, in fact, a trap. The Technic League pledged fealty to him and crowned him Numeria's new Black Sovereign. The Sovereign suddenly found himself in "command" of the League's considerable technological resources and in possession of an army of robotic gearsmen to protect his new capital. The Technic League immediately introduced him to all manner of strange narcotics and provided whatever the decadent pleasures the Black Sovereign demanded. Now Kevoth-Kul rules from a drug-induced haze and allows the secretive cabal great authority throughout the nation.

The suspicious nature of the Technic League reinforces members' insularity and usually precludes alliances with others. The Technic League and the Pathfinder Society stand in direct opposition. The former group is dedicated to the absolute control of lost knowledge and esoteric lore, while the latter's primary purpose is to discover and disseminate it. In 4704, the League convinced the drug addled Black Sovereign to burn the Pathfinder Lodge in Starfall to the ground. The Sovereign also proclaimed that any Pathfinder caught stealing secrets or technology would be hanged. The Pathfinder Society has since secretly relocated to Castle Urion and Hajoth Hakados, two Numerian settlements where the League's authority is not yet absolute.

INITIATION

Membership in the Technic League is limited to arcane spellcasters: primarily wizards and magi, but arcanists, alchemists, and sorcerers have always been welcome, as well as divine spellcasters of appropriate deities (such as worshipers of Brigh). In the early days of the Technic League, magically savvy rogues and other adventurers could find a place in the secret society, but through the years, their inclusion declined. Now only those with magical power are considered for induction into the upper echelons of the League. Bards can join but are often considered lesser members unless they prove successful at unlocking the secrets of new technological artifacts—a metric important to all in the Technic League.

The League does not actively recruit new members, except in cases where a highly knowledgeable candidate is discovered. Instead, individuals submit themselves for membership and the League considers whether each applicant possesses skills and abilities that can benefit the organization. The Technic League not only grants its members access to technology, but also provides a means to power and wealth, as well as a chance at a decadent lifestyle for those who attain a sufficient rank. Since its conquest of Starfall, the group has never had a shortage of those willing embrace its tenets, regardless of the cost. The majority of these applicants become servants or hirelings rather than full members—or can even become slaves, if they're not careful—but openings do occur on a semi-regular basis, as lesser members fall to misfortune. Even powerful, long-standing members occasionally obliterate themselves with experiments gone wrong or untimely accidents.

Formal admittance into the Technic League requires a sponsoring captain to submit the candidate's name before the Council of Captains. The candidate must demonstrate magic ability and is tested on her arcane knowledge. The council then votes in private on whether to accept the new member, though this is mostly a formality—rejecting another captain's hand-picked candidate is a sure route to a feud, and few captains would want an incompetent serving under them. Candidates who are rejected are sometimes offered lesser positions as hirelings and assistants and offered the promise of an opportunity for reconsideration, should they accomplish something noteworthy. Others are sent away; a few are killed because the council feels they have learned too much about the League while undergoing the selection process.

The most important part of the selection process, more important even than the council's approval, is the League's loyalty tests. These tests are designed by the initiate's sponsor, and they examine whether an aspirant is truly willing to put the League's interests—and those of his or her patron—above all else. This loyalty doesn't need to be selfless—the Technic League has no objection to the pursuit of personal power and wealth, so long as it never endangers the League as a whole. While even

assassination among the ranks of members is permissible if carried out discreetly, when it comes to outside threats to the League and its mission, a member should be prepared to do whatever is required by the organization, and pay whatever cost. As a result, loyalty tests are often (though not always) brutal and cruel by design, and may involve magical coercions, such as *geas*. Regardless of the specifics, a member of the Technic League must come out of the tests having proven herself willing to abandon nationality, faith, friendship, and morality itself should the League demand it. The Technic League routinely engages in blackmail, extortion, slavery, torture, and murder, and if a candidate is going to flinch at these activities, the council needs to know about this weakness prior to her induction.

Once admitted, new members are almost always granted accommodations in the Technic League's palace in Starfall and assigned to serve their sponsoring captain. This relationship is ideally more akin to mentorship than to actual servitude, though some captains hold on to their secrets more tightly than others. The initiates are watched closely and discreetly tested again to prevent excessive ambition and ensure that they are not merely clever infiltrators. In the Technic League, no one is ever above suspicion.

RANKS AND HIERARCHY

After being accepted into the League, members are granted accommodations in Starfall as well as a modest stipend. These benefits improve as the member advances in status. After "member," "captain" is the only standardized rank recognized throughout the League. Below the level of the Council of Captains, a member's standing depends largely on her personal power, achievements, and the approval of her patron captain. As such, titles are often quite loose, with captains assigning terms and ranks as they see fit. The information below is not absolute, but is rather an attempt to categorize the general structure observed within the League.

Agents, Assistants, and Hirelings: These individuals are attached to the Technic League, but not true members. An assistant may have been denied entrance into the League and given time to prove himself, or perhaps is simply in it for the coin. Many of them

Sidrah Imeruss

A THREAD OF SILVER

This thick, leather-bound book chronicles one of the earliest surveys of Silver Mount and its adjacent ruins. It far surpasses the value of *Pathfinder Chronicles Vol. 3* in respect to what it reveals about the Numerian ruins, as it partially describes some of Silver Mount's interior. *A Thread of Silver* was originally penned in 4515 AR by League member Lucius Worznik. An unidentified thief stole the volume in 4625. Over the years, the Technic League has dispatched many assassins to kill whoever owns it and return the book to the Technic League's libraries, only to discover that the book brought back to them is one of an unknown number of copies—the original has never been recovered. Yet, the League persists in sending agents across the Inner Sea to track down and recover any known copies, as well as to murder their owners.

This tenacity underscores the premium the Technic League places on technological knowledge and artifacts. A powerful artifact might garner a similar reaction, but the Technic League values relics no one fully understands every bit as much as its own knowledge and secrets. *A Thread of Silver* and its mechanical benefits are detailed in *Pathfinder Player Companion: Dungeoneer's Handbook*.

carry out the mundane drudgework of science and security, which is considered too boring for a full League member but too sensitive or specialized to be trusted to a mere slave. On occasion, agents are used as enforcers, spies, or assassins, and the best may even be loaned technological trinkets and tools for use in their missions. Because they are an exception to the League's rules about technology, agents being entrusted with artifacts are rigorously tested for loyalty before they are sent out in the field, and some are tagged with tracking devices.

Initiates: These are a brand new League members, still in their probationary period, and likely being observed and sometimes tested for both loyalty and a specific skill set. Initiates serve their sponsoring captain and any lieutenants, and they may observe and work with technology but are forbidden to own it. Advancement in rank occurs after a period of time set by their superiors.

Members: Most members still serve their patron captains, but may collect and own their own technology, run private experiments (so long as any findings are shared with their superiors), and have some level of autonomy. Members can and do shift allegiances between captains.

Commanders, Lieutenants, and Seconds: These are the most trusted subordinates of a Technic League captain—as well as their greatest threats, as it takes only a single fatal accident to turn a lieutenant into a captain. These members have great autonomy in their experiments and personal missions, directing League resources and lesser members toward a variety of ends. Some may be in charge of League activities in whole regions or settlements, keeping an eye on local governance and League interests. They may explore sites freely across Numeria, though the Silver Mount itself is still subject to certain restrictions imposed by the Council of Captains.

Captains: These few members are entitled to seats on the Council of Captains and have unfettered access to Silver Mount, as well as command of lesser Technic League members and agents—even those outside of their personal coteries. While captains are in charge of looking after League interests all across Numeria, most choose to stay in Starfall, where the concentration of resources and information is highest, and instead send lieutenants and seconds to keep an eye on matters of governance and the excavation of newly discovered wrecks. All captains have broad discretion for accessing League resources, including technology. Captains have routine access to the Black Sovereign and can heavily influence national policy decisions. They also have access to all manner of decadent pleasures, like the ones used to keep the Black Sovereign compliant.

MEMBERSHIP

Though the Technic League attempts to presents a unified front to the outside world, internal politics and rivalries seethe beneath the surface; one-upmanship, sabotage, and assassination are common. Most members join the Technic League for one reason: to increase their personal power. This motive manifests in a variety of ways, such as the need to attain wealth, gain the ability to pursue their often-depraved interests unconstrained by the morals of traditional society, or research esoteric knowledge simply for its own sake. Though members of sufficient rank are given time to pursue these interests, their obligations to the cabal are always expected to come first. All members are charged with protecting the League's secrets and monopoly over technology, assisting in controlling Numeria, and acquiring and disseminating knowledge throughout the League.

The mandated sharing of knowledge is a particularly fraught matter. It's rare to find friendships between members, or between low-ranking members and their supervising officers. Freely sharing knowledge is counterintuitive to many mages who seek power, and this is no different among members of the Technic League. In 4531, the Mage Mutiny exploded inside the Technic League as lower-ranked members rose up in protest., claiming (accurately) that supervising officers exploited their dangerous, difficult work and left them nothing to show for it. That era's Council of Captains sensed a major institutional schism was about to erupt and short-circuited it neatly. They decreed that while captains and their seconds were entitled to a certain amount of secrecy in their research, any significant results of these efforts must be shared with the rest of the League in a timely manner. Moreover, sharing discoveries with superiors would be the primary means of advancement within the society, and any lesser member who felt that her superior wasn't properly rewarding her research was welcome to switch her allegiance to a more appreciative captain. Only revealing secrets to those outside the League would be seen as a betrayal of trust and punished accordingly.

Thus did the League create an infrastructure that reinforced both institutional unity and solidarity against outside forces. The relationship between a member and her supervising officer is still fairly tense, as both parties attempt to alternately withhold and extort as much as they can from each other until the merits for promotion cannot be denied. The Council of Captains maintains a watchful eye on the supervising ranks to ensure they are being reasonably honest, lest the whole system fall apart. Ozmyn Zaidow is a perfect example of this system at work, as his recent series of new discoveries has catapulted him to the position of being the League's most influential captain.

Should a member die (research can be deadly at any rank), her supervising officer is quick to confiscate her notes and artifacts before another captain can. When a captain or commander dies, her peers descend upon her quarters like carrion birds. Her rooms and workshops are usually picked clean of any devices left unsecured or unhidden as soon as it is known the owner is dead. More than one supervising officer has devised a magical means to discern when one of her charges has met an untimely fate, so as to be the first to secure the subordinate's final work before anyone else can.

The primary responsibility of all members of any rank is to maintain the Technic League's stranglehold on technology, both in respect to actual knowledge and Numeria's many artifacts. To preserve the League's monopoly, every member is expected to kill when necessary and without hesitation. Any member found to knowingly leak information to outsiders or otherwise assist adventurers in their plundering can expect swift and terrible retribution.

GOVERNANCE OF NUMERIA

Though Numeria appears to be a monarchy, its true system of government is oligarchical despotism. Numeria is ruled by Kevoth-Kul, the Black Sovereign, but one of the nation's most poorly guarded secrets is that the Technic League heavily influences the Black Sovereign. The mages have his permission to run roughshod over the land and its people by royal decree—so long as the Sovereign and his cronies are kept entertained, unchallenged, and drugged into a state of euphoria.

In reality, the Technic League expends little effort influencing the country's governance except as it relates to the League's own interests. The Black Sovereign's officials—usually selected from the ruler's own friends and relations—handle the bulk of the country's administration, with the League stepping in only to provide advice on matters that interest them, as well as for the occasional show of force

to help keep the populace properly cowed. The League is careful never to overstep its bounds, however, for while the Black Sovereign may have degenerated into sloth and apathy, he's still a powerful figure—if properly roused, he and his barbarian horde might still be able to sweep the relatively small Technic League from the land.

The Council of Captains appoints certain members to watch over activities in key settlements and regions throughout Numeria. These appointments vary in their authority and their prestige. Captain Merisk Kaffaun enjoys an almost royal lifestyle and status in Chesed. Kannath, overseer of Aaramor, spends many of his days foiling assassination attempts (13 so far). Some settlements, like Castle Urion and Hajoth Hakados, are so filled with Mendevian crusaders or so close to the River Kingdoms that the Technic League's powers there are comparatively limited.

Technic League Commander

BRIGH

THE MINOR GODDESS BRIGH (BRY) IS A PUZZLING DEITY OF UNKNOWN ORIGIN, THE PATRON OF TECHNOLOGIES TOO COMPLEX FOR MOST FOLK TO UNDERSTAND. SHE IS THE GODDESS OF INVENTION, PARTICULARLY OF CREATING DEVICES THAT SEEM TO HAVE A LIFE OF THEIR OWN, SUCH AS CLOCKWORK CONSTRUCTS AND GOLEMS. BRIGH IS A PATIENT, CALM INVENTOR WILLING TO LEARN FROM MISTAKES AND CONSTANTLY TRYING TO CREATE AND TO IMPROVE HER WORK. SHE ENCOURAGES NEW DISCOVERIES IN DESIGN AND URGES HER FOLLOWERS TO SHARE THE KNOWLEDGE THEY HAVE GAINED THROUGH EXPERIMENTATION AND CAREFUL ENGINEERING. MANY DESIGNERS AND INVENTORS WHISPER HER NAME AS THEY STRUGGLE WITH NEW CREATIONS, HOPING SHE WILL BLESS THEIR WORK. AS A FRINGE GODDESS RESPONSIBLE FOR ESOTERIC AND EXPENSIVE CREATIONS, SHE HAS FEW WORSHIPERS, AND IS COMPLETELY UNKNOWN IN MANY PARTS OF THE WORLD.

Brigh is quiet and reserved, careful to not offend with casual words or gestures. However, she is not without emotion, and treasures the things her followers craft in her name. There is a special place in her mechanical heart for intelligent constructs, and anyone who treats these artificial beings like slaves or disposable playthings invites her wrath.

Also known as the Whisper in Bronze, Brigh communicates with her followers like a mentor or a learned professor, dispensing advice, proofs, and data to push the limits of her audience's understanding, with the hope of inspiring her followers to greater and more impressive creations. Brigh is coolly distant even with her own worshipers, as she doesn't want to show favoritism. Many of her worshipers prefer the company of tools and machines to other living beings, however, and thus don't consider this aloofness unusual.

Brigh is so inscrutable that even her own priesthood maintains several theories regarding her origin. Some claim she was once mortal and obtained godhood through some unknown means. Others preach she was originally a created being that moved beyond the faculties of a normal construct and gained a spark of life and divinity. The followers who believe she was once a living person say that she was a talented prodigy studying alchemy and clockwork. By uniting disparate theories of natural life and construct creation, she was able to seamlessly fuse mechanical parts with her body, creating a composite form that gave her incredible powers of strength, agility, and mental calculation. Much as the god Irori's pursuit of self-perfection allowed him to transcend his mortal form, her endeavors transformed her into something on the border of mortal and deity—perhaps a mythic being or a demigod. Devotees of this theory suggest that her mortal name was lost during the centuries she spent in isolation, creating and perfecting her dual form, explaining why there is no record of such a woman, or that name, in any mortal academy or lists of inventors' pupils.

Brigh's philosophy is that you should build upon the work of others and share your work so others can improve upon it after you are gone. Your creations are your children, your legacy. Paying attention to details is critical; you should identify a problem, plot a course of action to correct that problem, and try a different course if the first one doesn't work. Brigh understands physical and emotional needs such as food, sex, and friendship, but thinks people shouldn't make such base needs their top priority.

"NEED SPAWNS INVENTION, BUT IMAGINATION GIVES RISE TO NEED."
—LOGIC OF DESIGN

The Whisper in the Bronze is a proponent of all invention, even the invention of destructive things, for even a dangerous tool can be used for creative purposes. She opposes destroying information, as doing so sets back the advancement of technology for everyone. If a person's research leads in a direction she believes to be dangerous or immoral, however, that person is free to stop pursuing such research.

Brigh appears to be a slender human woman made of bronze clockwork. Sometimes she appears as a beautiful woman wearing clockwork armor with a bronze skullcap. It is unclear which of these is her true form, or whether both are different aspects of her true self: one of her machine nature and one of her living nature. When Brigh appears in her clockwork form, she has been known to open a cavity in her chest and draw out perfectly crafted mechanisms that she then bestows on other creatures and creations. She can also adjust, add, and remove devices from her internal workings—some removed devices inherit part of her will and function as independent creatures. Likewise, in her living form she can alter parts of her armor to change their abilities or transform them into components for clockwork weapons.

In art, she is typically depicted in either her living of her clockwork form, though she is sometimes represented by a bronze mask hovering in place. Some temples craft a clockwork shell in her likeness and use it as an object of veneration. Gnome artists depict her proportioned like a gnome instead of a human, with long eyebrows and hair made of multicolored metallic wires.

When Brigh is pleased, damaged gears spontaneously repair themselves, mirrors acquire a bronze color, constructs whisper words of encouragement, the smell of grease or gunpowder wafts through the air, and worshipers acquire sudden insight into their current projects. When she is angered, alchemical reagents explode, mindless constructs go berserk, intelligent constructs rebel, grease and oil spontaneously catch fire, quills break, inkpots spill, and innocuous materials become irritants.

Brigh is neutral, and her portfolio is invention and clockwork. She has recently been expanding her clockwork aspect to include measuring and calculating time (such as by using timepieces and mechanical calculating devices). Her weapon is the light hammer. Her holy symbol is a bronze, feminine mask with a rune engraved into the forehead. Her domains are Artifice, Earth, Fire, and Knowledge. Most of her worshipers are humans, but she has many gnome, half-elven, and half-orc followers. Much of her church is concentrated in Alkenstar and Numeria. Many intelligent constructs consider her their patron deity. Her priests are primarily clerics, although the church has a few inquisitors who hunt down rampaging constructs, people who allow their constructs to go rogue, and those who abuse intelligent constructs.

Typical worshipers of Brigh are experts who craft with their hands, especially blacksmiths, jewelers, gemcutters, toymakers, and inventors. Some alchemists more interested in pure research than the practicality of their inventions worship her, and their experimentation yields many novel items, including the occasional useful one such as a tanglefoot bag or tindertwig. Those inventors who pray to her see her as the personification of their art—a human-like shape that has transcended its human flaws.

Worshipers usually wear a toothed gear as jewelry, and some carry sets of miniature tools as ritual objects when full-sized versions would be unnecessary or impractical. Adventurers who serve Brigh often wear helmets in the shape of her holy mask, decorated with bronze accents (although most still use steel armor, as it's stronger than bronze).

Worship services mix bells, the sounds of music boxes, and the recitation of formulas (such as the inverse relation between gas volume, pressure, and temperature, or the quantities of metals in a salt bath needed to produce electricity). Offerings to the goddess are made during these ceremonies and usually consist of fine oils, rare materials, well-used tools, and demonstrations of new inventions.

Brigh has little interest in mortal marriage or families. However, she recognizes that her worshipers may need such things, and that talent for intellect and invention are often inherited, so if a mortal wants to devote energy to such matters, she accepts this. Even offspring with no talent for study can be useful for cleaning work areas, taking dictation, transcribing notes, or performing grunt labor necessary for building complex devices—assuming they old enough to do so safely and without risk of interfering with an experiment.

TEMPLES AND SHRINES

There are few temples to Brigh, and most are built like workshops, with many places for crafting and tinkering. Many include a place where visitors can purchase items crafted by the temple, or warehouse space for items destined to be sent elsewhere. One of the largest temples to Brigh is in Alkenstar, as that city is full of engineers, inventors, and technically minded artisans. The head of a temple is called the High Clockmother or High Clockfather, and is usually the most knowledgeable priest at that location (if not the most powerful).

Shrines to Brigh are much more common than temples, and many workshops and laboratories have a bronze mask or large gear mounted on the wall to honor her.

A PRIEST'S ROLE

Priests are expected to devote much of their lives to research. For most, this means experimenting and inventing in a workshop or laboratory. The luckiest of these have wealthy sponsors who provide funds and supplies, allowing them to devote all of their time to their work; many temples accept donations for this purpose or sell trinkets and useful items to provide funding for their resident priests.

A few priests pursue interests that require fieldwork or exploration. Such activities might include searching the records of old civilizations for hints about their metallurgy techniques or lost technology, looking for higher-quality sources of alchemical materials, or taking advantage of natural phenomena that cannot easily be reproduced by mortal hands (such as an area known for unusual magnetism, pockets of magma, or frequent lightning strikes). These trips are usually followed by a period of time in a settlement where the priests refine their experimental methodology or expand their notes into monographs that can then be shared with other researchers.

Other priests of Brigh become peddlers or tinkers, selling their own inventions or those created by others, spreading the word about how these devices can make life easier, more efficient, or more entertaining. These peddler-priests sell only items that work (although their creations sometimes make the tasks they complete only slightly easier than if the task had been done by hand). Brigh's priests loathe quacks, charlatans, and sellers of fraudulent goods. Of course, priest-peddlers of the Whisper sometimes sell controversial items themselves. Some create traps for protecting doors; more powerful (and expensive) variants of crossbows or firearms; clockwork spies; or crank-powered, electrical torture devices, selling such goods to banks, armies, thieves' guilds, and tyrants.

Brigh's clerics are usually trained in Knowledge (engineering), Craft (alchemy, carpentry, clocks, glass, leather, or locks), or Profession (architect, engineer, miner, or scribe). Those who perform dangerous research are usually trained in Heal as well, in case something goes wrong and they or their assistants are injured. Adventuring clerics usually have ranks in skills such as Craft (weapons) or Disable Device as well.

Because their interests are so specialized, priests of Brigh usually don't have active roles in their communities (much in the same way that priests of Nethys devote themselves to magic and rarely interact with local merchants and farmers). The exceptions are in Alkenstar, where the clergy are heavily involved in the development and manufacture of firearms, and Numeria, where they catalog and attempt to identify the artifacts scavenged from the surrounding lands. Brigh's faith is so small that outside of those two technology-minded lands, few people have ever heard of her, and fewer still have met one of her priests. Most priests have no interest in proselytizing, and a significant number actively avoid discussing religion with layfolk.

Each morning, a priest typically rises, eats a simple and efficient meal, and refreshes her mind for the day's work. Many are so driven that they work long hours and forget to eat or sleep, and must be reminded to do so by a spouse, assistant, or timepiece. The use of stimulants to increase productivity or waking hours is common. The priests are used to erratic schedules and may become frustrated by others who prefer a more normal routine. More practical folk say these inventors are "married to the Whisper," in much the way that new lovers are so obsessed with each other that they forget all else. Those who work in a group environment (such as a temple-funded workshop) are used to consulting with others about problems, and long, enthusiastic, and speculative talks between colleagues often contribute to late hours. Those who have larger roles in their communities might work on projects such as better ballistas to protect the town, more efficient ways to stabilize mine tunnels, or experimental clinics offering free (and potentially unorthodox) healing.

There is no formal dress for the clergy, and since Brigh's faith is made up of practical people, most wear a leather work coat, accented with bronze buttons and clasps. Somewhere on the coat is usually a large button in the shape of Brigh's mask. Often a pair of oversized leather-bound goggles and a close-fitting leather cap, which double as protective laboratory gear, complete the outfit. Priests use this outfit for work as well as worship, and it often acquires a respectable assortment of scorch marks, acid burns, and patched areas over time. A priest might add a decorative badge showing her field of interest or indicating a significant invention or accolade given to her by other inventors.

HOLIDAYS

As Brigh is a minor goddess, no months in the standard Golarion calendar are named for her. She has no set holidays, though individual temples make note of the anniversaries of important discoveries and inventions, particularly if they took place at that location or are attributed to a prominent member of that community. These remembrances take place at a convenient time within a few days of the event's actual anniversary. Temples usually give a nod to local holidays and those of friendly deities if the holidays have some aspect that's of interest to the church. For example, the faithful honor Abadar's Taxfest (performing complex calculations to make sure there is no inaccuracy in the taxes they owe), Andoran's Wrights of Augustana (praising the math and engineering necessary to build large ships), and Sarenrae's Sunwrought Festival (potentially crafting the fireworks).

APHORISMS

As Brigh's followers are always attempting to expand the frontiers of knowledge—not an easy road to walk—many of the faith's common phrases are used to inspire hope and determination.

Invention Is Immortality: Many followers of Brigh are so devoted to their craft that they cannot maintain a family and never have children. The church teaches that for such people, their inventions are their children, their work is their legacy, and allowing others to learn and use their discoveries is as good as passing on a family name. This aphorism is a rebuttal against criticism for their monomania—in the eyes of the church, some people are meant to have children, while others are meant to discover how to turn iron into steel or invent a spring that can't be overwound.

Question, Propose, Test: The basis of understanding the world is to think of a question, pose an answer to it, and find a way to test whether or not that answer is true. Each of these concepts is part of a "perfect triangle" of understanding; all three parts are necessary and interdependent. Questioning without proposals or testing is mere philosophy. An answer can't exist without a question, and an answer without testing is mere speculation. Testing without a question or hypothesis is dangerous experimentation.

Share What You Know: Every discovery since the dawn of civilization has allowed later inventors to create even greater things than those who came before them. Hiding knowledge from the world is like stealing from starving, future minds. The church doesn't expect all researchers and inventors to publicly disclose everything, but they should document their work so that others can benefit from it (even if only posthumously).

HOLY TEXT

The official book of the church is *Logic of Design*, much of which is presented as an essay, or perhaps the transcription of a lecture, covering the basic ideas of innovation, experimentation, documentation, and discovery. Later sections provide a cursory overview of the fields of metallurgy, electricity, physics (particularly in relation to motion), and stonemasonry, as if the book were intended to be a primer for a series of university courses. Large parts of these later sections have a different writing style than the first part, as if the general concepts of these chapters were sketched out by the original author and filled in by students or other researchers. Very little of the book is presented as religious dogma; instead, the contents within are cast as information established through research and study.

RELATIONS WITH OTHER RELIGIONS

Brigh maintains a careful distance from other deities, taking care not to antagonize them or get in the middle of feuds. She is fairly close with Abadar, as he admires the fruits of her invention, particularly items that improve construction methods, allow for faster counting and calculation, and facilitate record keeping. She looks favorably on Torag because of his focus on creation and work with the forge. She is on good terms with Cayden Cailean, who appreciates the science of brewing. She and Norgorber have collaborated in the past on certain aspects of alchemical research, though his unwillingness to share information has soured this relationship. She dislikes Rovagug, as there is no creation in him, only destruction. Of the major deities, she is closest with Shelyn, despite having very few common interests aside from a focus on artistic creation. Brigh has a close working relationship with other non-evil deities that share the Artifice domain, namely the empyreal lords Bharnarol and Eldas.

While Brigh herself has opinions regarding the other deities, she makes no rules regarding whom her worshipers can associate with, as the free pursuit of new knowledge can lead to strange but ultimately beneficial partnerships.

NEW SPELLS

Brigh's clerics can spontaneously cast *make whole*, *mending*, and *soothe construct*[UM]. Her inquisitors can learn *mending* as a 1st-level spell, *make whole* as a 2nd-level spell, and *soothe construct*[UM] as a 3rd-level spell. Her clerics also have access to the following spell.

School illusion (glamer); **Level** cleric 2, sorcerer/wizard 2 (Brigh)
Casting Time 1 standard action
Components V, S
Range touch
Target construct touched
Duration 10 minute/level (D)

You make the target construct appear to be a living creature of flesh and bone, regardless of its actual materials. You can make it seem 1 foot shorter or taller, and appear thin, fat, or anywhere in between. Its bodily configuration does not change; for example, a centaur-like construct looks like a centaur rather than a human. The extent of the apparent change (such as flesh color, hair color, apparent age, and so on) is up to you.

The spell does not provide the abilities or mannerisms of the chosen form, nor does it alter the perceived tactile or audible properties of the construct. If you use this spell to create a disguise, the construct gains a +10 bonus on the Disguise check. A creature that interacts with the glamer receives a Will save to recognize it as an illusion.

PLANAR ALLIES

Many of Brigh's divine servants were once mortal inventors recreated in "perfect" mechanical forms, and she treats them as her children or younger siblings. These beings have the same statistics as they did in life, except that they have the construct type and the clockwork subtype. Most of her other servitors are intelligent clockwork creatures and golems. Her herald is Latten Mechanism (see page 84). Her most frequently summoned servitors are the following.

Karapek: This dark-haired male alchemist is made of bronze, with large hands and a back reinforced with struts of polished steel. He has knowledge regarding constructs and flesh golem construction, and is a prolific writer on theoretical topics that cannot be realized with current levels of technology. He sees himself as an ambassador between living creatures and sentient constructs, and is loathe to attack intelligent living or construct creatures.

Salometa: This serious-faced female inventor is made of a dull, lead-like metal, lit by an eerie interior green glow visible from her eyes and mouth. She is able to emit this energy like a breath weapon, using it to burn opponents or cure certain diseases and parasitic infestations. This energy can also separate metals into their component materials (such as bronze into copper and tin) and even disintegrate small quantities of metal.

OBEDIENCE

The following describes the ritual a worshiper of Brigh must perform to take full advantage of the Deific Obedience feat found on page 210 of *Pathfinder Campaign Setting: Inner Sea Gods*, as well as the boons for the evangelist, exalted, and sentinel prestige classes.

CUSTOMIZED SUMMON LIST

Brigh's priests can use summon monster spells to summon the following creatures in addition to the normal creatures listed in the spells. The creatures below gain the extraplanar subtype but otherwise have the normal statistics for a creature of their kind.

Summon Monster I
Clockwork spy (*Pathfinder RPG Bestiary 3* 58)
Summon Monster IV
Clockwork servant (*Bestiary 3* 56)
Summon Monster VI
Clockwork soldier (*Bestiary 3* 57)

Obedience: While reciting formulas from *Logic of Design*, you must craft a new creation, continue work on an elaborate device or object, or disassemble an existing creation to see how it works. Share the knowledge you discover while working on this project. Gain a +4 sacred bonus on Disable Device checks.

EVANGELIST BOONS

1: Voice of Bronze (Sp) *jury-rig*UC 3/day, *fox's cunning* 2/day, *sands of time*UM 1/day

2: Living Construct (Su) You can affect constructs as if they were living creatures. Once per day, you can target a construct with a spell or spell-like ability, and the spell resolves as if its creature type were humanoid.

3: Frozen Time (Su) You gain the ability to halt time. You can use *time stop* as a spell-like ability once per day.

EXALTED BOONS

1: Creator (Sp) *crafter's fortune*APG 3/day, *make whole* 2/day, *minor creation* 1/day

2: Protected by the Machine (Su) Your body is as resistant as a construct. You gain a +2 sacred bonus on saves against effects that cause ability damage, ability drain, fatigue, exhaustion, energy drain, or nonlethal damage.

3: Inspired Crafting (Su) When crafting magic items while adventuring, you can devote 4 hours each day to creation and take advantage of the full amount of time spent crafting instead of netting only 2 hours' worth of work. In addition, you can use *fabricate* once per day as a spell-like ability. Though you can't create magic items with the *fabricate* spell, you can use it to create items that you later enhance magically.

SENTINEL BOONS

1: Bronze Warrior (Sp) *crafter's curse*APG 3/day, *heat metal* 2/day, *haste* 1/day

2: Constructed Form (Su) As a swift action, you gain DR 3/— for a number of rounds per day equal to your Hit Dice. These rounds need not be consecutive.

3: Call to Battle (Su) Once per day as a full-round action, you can summon a clockwork golem (*Pathfinder RPG Bestiary 2* 137). The golem follows your commands perfectly for 1 minute for each hit die you possess before vanishing.

UNEARTHED TREASURES

We left Hajoth Hakados shortly after dawn and struck out northwest across the Numerian plains. "I've lived in the wastelands all my youth. I know its secrets," I said. "Most travelers follow the riverbank, a longer route that leaves them easy prey for bandits. We'll cut across the plains and cross the river near its end."

Eirian made no response. By the time the sun reached its zenith, I had learned that my traveling companion spoke only when necessary. At first I found her silence eerie, almost grating. I offered up observations on the land, commenting on familiar features and relaying hunting stories from my childhood. She listened in silence, even showing no reaction to my best story—that of the time I went hunting and was in turn hunted by a starving worg.

Eirian made no comment at the end of my tale. With a touch of reproach, I said, "Most people find that story exciting."

"How can it be exciting when you obviously survived?"

I had no argument for that.

As evening fell, we came upon a stretch of broken earth. Misshapen mounds stood between gullies that cut across the ground. A greasy haze hung over the area like fog. Creaks and whirs sounded in the distance. The remaining sunlight glinted off bits of bright metal stuck among the jagged rocks. I hesitated here.

"You said you knew how to travel the wastelands," Eirian said. "Yet you seem uneasy."

EIRIAN WEARS THIS CONSTANTLY, BUT SHE MOSTLY KEEPS IT TUCKED INTO HER JACKET.

"My people distrust technology," I said. "We avoid these places, places where we might encounter mechanical creatures or technological artifacts. I admit I have little familiarity with such areas."

"I can guide us through."

I glanced at Eirian. She stared serenely toward the horizon. "You said you are a scavenger of ruins. Have you been here before?"

"Yes," she replied. "Many times. It was a village ages ago, built to excavate the land. No one has lived here for centuries, but some of the structures remain."

"Then this place must hold no more secrets for you."

She shook her head. "The ground always holds secrets. Quiet earth can unfold and reveal treasures beneath. Machinery buried in stone tombs can dig its way out after thousands of years. Even a well-picked site can hold new prizes days, weeks, or months later. Some say that a machine lies beneath this land and sometimes it churns, trying to dig itself out."

"I can see why so many androids would stay in Hajoth Hakados then, despite the danger. There's no need to move farther away if you can always scavenge new items in old sites."

She fixed me with her calm gaze, and now that I knew to look for it, I could see the metallic sheen where the sun caught her eyes in the right way. "Not all androids are scavengers."

Her tone made it impossible to tell if I'd offended her. I started to speak, but she held up a hand. "I recommend we rest here and strike out again in the morning."

"Agreed."

We made our camp, rough as it was—two bedrolls on either side of a small fire that we used to heat dried meat and some withered vegetables in water to make a thin soup. We ate the meager meal with hard rolls and then covered the fire to so as not to attract unwanted attention.

"Are you still certain you wish to accompany me?" I asked as we ate.

Eirian nodded. "You have been marked by Brigh. I go where you go."

"My people might not be as welcoming to you as I have been." I took a drink from my waterskin. "They still mightily distrust technology."

"You hold no such belief."

My gaze dropped to the metal cuff on my wrist. The ache had faded, but the cuff still resisted all our efforts to remove it. I grimaced. "I have traveled much and seen wonders my parents never dreamed of. I accept some technology and innovation may be necessary. You can't always live by tradition."

After a moment of quiet, she asked, "Will they harm me?"

"No," I said. "I will speak for you. But they may not allow you inside the village."

"Then I will wait outside until the Whisper in the Bronze guides me elsewhere."

Her placidity lent a strange weight to her words. I could easily picture her waiting outside my village, through rain and fog and deep chill, letting the months passed until I set out again.

I hoped Brigh would guide her elsewhere soon.

I drove sticks into the ground around our campsite and strung thread between them. Eirian hung a few shards of metal from the string, a rudimentary alarm should anyone disturb us in the night. I wrapped myself in my bedroll while Eirian found a comfortable place to rest.

I had almost drifted off when I heard a sound—a repeated thumping that was so low and distant I hadn't heard it over the our conversation and movement. Now that we were still, I could sense it on the very edge of my hearing: *clank clank clank.*

"Do you hear that?"

"I do," Eirian replied after a moment. "I cannot tell what it is."

"Nor can I." I sat up in the dark, listening. "I don't think it's getting closer."

"I agree. Perhaps we should investigate in the morning."

Part of me wanted to head out into the night and track down the source of the mysterious sound, but it remained distant. There was no reason to investigate right at the moment, in the dark.

"Very well. In the morning."

Eirian sat silently, watching over the camp as I rested. Sleep eluded me, though. I stared up at familiar stars and listened to the far-off clanking, like a mechanical heart beating in the night. The moon was almost overhead when I finally closed my eyes and let sleep overtake me.

My people call the areas of devastation in Numeria "rendlands." Rendlands can be as small as a hut or as large as a town. They pop up like mushrooms over the face of our land, marking spots where fragments fell from the sky during the Rain of Stars. Explorers, researchers, and scavengers dig up these areas from time to time, hunting for bits of skymetal or artifacts from distant worlds, though most of these places have been stripped clean. This rendland's proximity to Hajoth Hakados made me suspect that it had been excavated many times before.

We picked our way across the landscape. Craters and narrow ravines scarred the ground, making for treacherous footing. We were only a few minutes into the area when a tremor tore open the ground near my feet. I leaped back and managed to hold my balance as a two-foot-deep rift opened before us. The ground stilled again, as if nothing had happened.

Eirian put a hand on my arm. "Are you hurt?"

I shook my head. "Let's keep moving."

IF WE WOULDN'T HAVE COME BY, THIS LITTLE GUY WOULD STILL BE STUCK

We pressed on through a barren region of trembling earth. More than once I was almost knocked to the ground. Soon, though, the tremors subsided and the wreckage of old stone buildings came into view. The *clank clank clank* grew steadily louder. Eirian left her hammer at her belt. I wasn't sure whether she ever used the weapon in battle or if it served only as a symbol of her faith.

Given a choice, I'd rather fight with my hands than use a blade. I flexed my left hand, testing its mobility. I still felt a twinge when moving it, but overall noticed no change in its range of motion. If anything, the metal cuff added stability and weight to my forearm. I hastened my pace, moving a half-step ahead of Eirian.

She stayed behind me as we threaded our way through the ruins. Most of the buildings looked to have been dwellings— simple stone structures that had mostly collapsed. Some remained intact, though, even to the roofs. Piles of rubble blocked what once had been streets. We stepped carefully as we approached the source of the noise.

The thump never grew unbearably loud, but the sound seemed sharper, more distinct, as we approached a gully. I motioned for Eirian to slow.

I sprinted ahead, not caring about stealth. If danger lurked in the gully, I would come upon it fast and overwhelm it. I slowed and paused for only a moment at the edge of the gully, and at the sight of what lay within I jumped down without hesitation.

A tumble of fallen rocks blocked the gully a few feet to the north. The *clank clank clank* echoed clearly down the earthen canal. A mobile metal device beat itself relentlessly against the stone barrier, its body clanging against the stone.

Eirian arrived at the edge of the ravine and peered down at me. She held her hammer in one hand. "I am glad to see you have some means of defending yourself," I said.

She looked at her hammer then back at me. "Brigh comes to my aid in times of need. What is that?"

I approached the metal creature. A single yellow eye glowed from the center of its round body. A pair of treads revolved beneath it, rolling across fallen rocks but never gaining traction. Four spindly, multi-jointed appendages sprouted from its body. The whole apparatus would have fit in my large pack.

"I've seen creatures like this before, on the plains." I walked cautiously around the whirring device. "I believe it's a robot."

Eirian landed lightly behind me. "Like the gearsmen of Starfall." Her voice carried a tone I was coming to associate with discomfort.

"I don't think this one belongs to the Technic League, judging by how long it's been here." I pointed. "That limb is pinned under the rocks. Maybe it was passing through and got caught in a rockslide. This area is unstable."

I watched the little robot struggle, its limbs pinned beneath the rocks and its treads trying to move them. Eirian spoke again. "Perhaps we should assist it."

I started to shake my head. The robot looked to pose little threat, small as it was. But we knew nothing of its origin or purpose, and it seemed safer not to interfere.

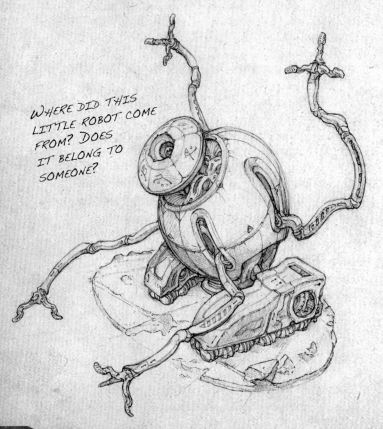

WHERE DID THIS LITTLE ROBOT COME FROM? DOES IT BELONG TO SOMEONE?

At almost at the same instance, Eirian and I noticed the markings on the robot's round head. We both took a step forward.

"The runes," Eirian said, pointing.

"They match the ones on my cuff."

"My cuff."

"Of course." I dropped to one knee next to the trapped robot and held my arm next to its markings.

"They're identical," Eirian said. I nodded in agreement. A band of etched panels surrounded the robot's eye, and each one contained a rune matching one on my—I mean, Eirian's—cuff.

"If this robot has something to do with the cuff," I said, "we might somehow use it to get this thing off my arm."

"Do you have a plan?"

I shook my head. "I may be more comfortable with technology than my people, but that doesn't mean I understand it. Isn't this more your specialty?"

Eirian examined the robot. We tried tapping my cuff against the robot, touching the matching runes together. Nothing happened. The cuff stayed firmly wrapped around my wrist.

"I've reached the limits of my knowledge," Eirian finally said. "Whatever the connection between this robot and my cuff is, I can't tell."

"Then maybe we should release it," I said. "It seems to be trying to get somewhere. Flocks of birds fly from Mendev to Qadira in the summer then return the following season. Maybe this robot is on its way back to its home."

"You think if we follow it, we could learn about its origin?"

"We might even meet its maker. And the maker of the cuff."

"It's pointed toward your village."

"Better still. Now, how to free it."

The rocks crushing the robot's limbs and body were piled all around. I hunted for an item I could use as a lever. Eirian tried to lift one of the rocks off the pile but could barely shift it. I hurried back to help her.

"I don't see anything I can use for a tool," I said. I grasped the rock and tried to move it. "Perhaps together we can—"

The rock moved so suddenly that Eirian and I both staggered off-balance. It slipped from our grasp and tumbled down the pile, glancing off my ankle as it did. I winced as a bruise blossomed.

"Sorry," I said. "I didn't realize it would come loose so fast."

"It shouldn't have." Eirian bent to examine the stone. "It's much too heavy."

"You must have loosened it."

"I did not." She straightened and stepped back. "Try to move the next one."

I put my hands on either side of the topmost stone, even though I could tell it would be too heavy for me to move. The rocks were larger than my head, rough and gritty with the same tawny hue as the wastelands. I gripped the rock tightly and tried to lift it.

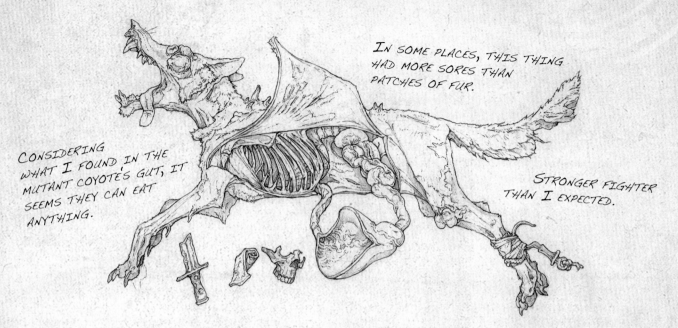

IN SOME PLACES, THIS THING HAD MORE SORES THAN PATCHES OF FUR.

CONSIDERING WHAT I FOUND IN THE MUTANT COYOTE'S GUT, IT SEEMS THEY CAN EAT ANYTHING.

STRONGER FIGHTER THAN I EXPECTED.

To my surprise, the rock shifted. I tightened my grip and as I did, I felt the cuff around my wrist tighten. My arm tingled as if the muscles within all contracting at once. I lifted the stone—it wobbled in my uneven grip, but the strength in my cuffed arm allowed me to pull the stone off the pile and toss it to the side.

"It's the cuff," I said to Eirian.

She received this news with her usual placid demeanor. "Then clear the rest away."

I set to work, and in a short time I'd removed nearly all the rocks. As I lifted the last stone, the robot pulled its spindly limbs free. It shot forward, climbing over the rubble and hauling itself up the ravine wall like a spider.

"After it!" I barked.

Eirian and I scrambled to follow the robot. Once it reached the surface, it retracted its limbs and began trundling along on its treads.

"It's certainly on some sort of mission," I said as we sprinted to catch up with the robot. Eirian nodded. Once we were abreast of the little machine, we slowed to a walk. Though it maintained a steady pace, the robot was not overly quick.

We followed the robot for a while, and though I watched it carefully for signs of hostility, the robot seemed completely unaware of our presence. I admired its ingenuity. When it encountered rough terrain or obstacles, its limbs extended and it clambered over the impediment or brushed its path free. In smooth areas it drew its appendages back in and rolled along on its tread. Eirian and I had no trouble keeping up with the robot, though from time to time we had to clamber over a rocky barrier.

"Once we get onto the plains," I said, "we'll travel more smoothly."

"I'm interested in seeing how it gets across the river."

I smiled at that thought.

We'd been traveling for almost an hour, and I believed we were close to the edge of the rendland. The sun was still early in the sky. I entertained thoughts of stopping for a midday meal once we were back on the plains.

As I tried to think of a way to keep the robot from getting too far ahead of us while we stopped to eat or camp, a scream jolted me out of my reverie. Eirian and I spun around.

We saw nothing. The scream came from the west, from beyond the piles of scrap and stone. The tremulous howl of some wild animal cut the scream in half. I touched Eirian's shoulder. "Follow the robot. I'll catch up."

"You're putting yourself at risk."

"Someone needs help. Go, I'll find you."

Eirian strode after the robot. I sprinted, threading my way through the ruin. The animal howls continued, raising the hairs on the back of my neck. The howling chorus was shrill and sharp, sometimes disturbingly like human laughter. I had traveled many places in my life and met many fearsome creatures. This could easily be a trap, but I couldn't risk abandoning a traveler in need.

The path curved around a mass of broken stone and I slowed as I followed it. A clear space lay within the ruin, perhaps an old town square. A decrepit building with a wide stone porch across the clearing might have been a town hall, maybe even a temple.

The howls had died away to a solitary *yipyipyip* that pierced the midday silence. Around the bend, bodies lay crumpled on the ground like so many piles of scrap. Oozing blood formed puddles on the ground. Three bodies, dead and unmoving, and a fourth rushing toward me with slavering jaws open. I caught sight of one gleaming eye surrounded by swollen green pustules and a set of overlarge, jagged fangs and then it was on me, teeth seeking the meat of my arm.

I braced myself and swung my arm wide as the animal leaped for me. Its lean, gray-furred body arched like a bow, its front paws tight together, its bushy tail curving between its hind legs. I smashed my arm into its yellow muzzle and the creature flew sideways, yipping. It landed on its side and rolled but came up on its feet immediately and charged me again.

I squatted to steady myself and drove quick, successive punches into the animal's breast when it leaped for me again. My knuckles bruised on some sort of bony carapace covered in patchy fur. I'd seen coyotes on the plains before—scavengers, mainly, but also hunters of small prey like rabbits and ground birds. But no coyote I'd ever seen had bulbous growths on its hide, or that thick of a breastbone. And this beast was twice as tall as an ordinary coyote, nearly the size of a wolf.

Growing up in Numeria, I had seen a few animals mutated by the technological waste that lurked in the soil. Here, it seemed, I had met another.

The coyote stumbled sideways, then spun around and nipped at my arm. Its overlarge teeth ripped long furrows through skin and muscle. I grunted in pain, and within me the slumbering bear began to wake.

When the coyote charged again, I met its shrill bay with a guttural roar. My blood rushed like a river in my ears. I dove forward and smashed my shoulder into the coyote's chest, driving it back. Its paws skidded, black nails digging into the earth. It tried to rear up on its hind legs, scrabbling at my gut with its front paws. I flipped it to the side, smashing it onto the ground. It yowled horrifically and rolled over, struggling to balance on three legs. I'd hurt one of the back paws.

As I reached to grab the fur ruff around its neck, the coyote snapped swift as a rattlesnake. It got my hand between its jaws and clamped down. I felt its teeth sink past flesh and scrape the bones of my hand and I howled in pain and rage. I pulled the beast closer to me with my injured hand and drove my other fist into its ribs, over and over. The bones splintered and cracked under my enhanced strength. The runes on the back of the cuff glowed with blue energy.

The coyote released my hand and tried to squirm past me, yipping in pain. I couldn't let it get away—with the injuries I'd dealt so far, it would die a slow and painful death in the wastelands. I flung myself onto the animal's back, letting my weight bring it to the ground. Its injured leg gave way and it went down baying. I pulled myself along its body until I got both hands around its neck. I could do little more than hold on with my mangled right hand, but my left hand had more than enough strength to break the coyote's neck. Its body went limp beneath mine.

I got to my feet slowly, rocking with dizziness. My hand throbbed and blood dripped from my fingertips. I took a moment to examine the coyote's body. Beneath its fur I found patches of bony growth reinforcing its hide along with more

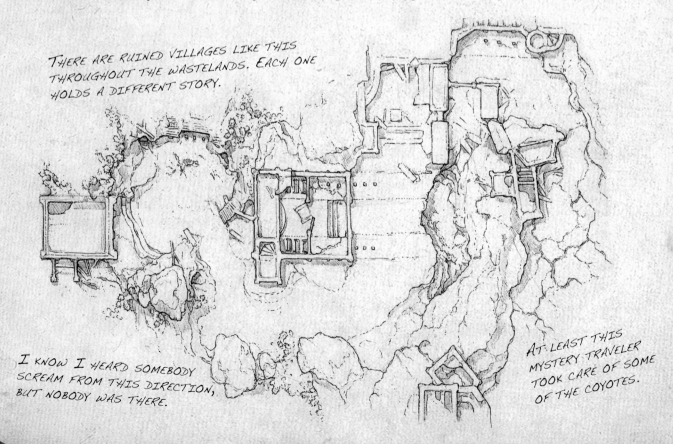

THERE ARE RUINED VILLAGES LIKE THIS THROUGHOUT THE WASTELANDS. EACH ONE HOLDS A DIFFERENT STORY.

I KNOW I HEARD SOMEBODY SCREAM FROM THIS DIRECTION, BUT NOBODY WAS THERE.

AT LEAST THIS MYSTERY TRAVELER TOOK CARE OF SOME OF THE COYOTES.

ROBOTS

Unlike androids, robots are wholly mechanical constructions. This is not to say that robots are mindless automatons. On the contrary, many display uncommon intelligence. Most can talk, though they often choose not to. People have a hard time understanding a robot's motivations, and an even more difficult time controlling these machines.

The origin of robots remains a mystery. Though it seems clear they arrived in the same vessel that broke apart in the Rain of Stars, the given many types of robots, it's difficult to know what any one of them was created for. One humanoid robot might be made for heavy lifting, while another might be a skilled warrior. Though a number of things can be inferred from a robot's appearance, judging one strictly by its external design is a sure way to put oneself at a disadvantage.

Though robots exist in a variety of forms and display numerous powers, they share certain common abilities. Robots' thick metal shells afford them considerable protection, and some manifest energy-based force fields for extra defense. Their built-in weapons can fire projectiles, energy beams, or even plasma. The complex technology that constitutes a robot keeps the secrets of its construction well hidden, but also makes it vulnerable to electrical attacks.

Residents of Numeria treat robots with extreme caution. Though some robots are accepted as a common sight, such as the gearsmen of Starfall, most Numerians understand that robots are dangerous and unpredictable.

---

patches of pustules. Some had broken open and oozed a foul-smelling green liquid onto its fur. A cursory examination showed that the other three bodies were similarly mutated. I shuddered as I prodded their cooling bodies.

What I couldn't figure out was what had killed the other coyotes. Thin puncture wounds marred their corpses, the kind dealt by a blade. A rapier, perhaps, or a thin short sword. The wounds were too deep for a dagger. I looked around but saw no evidence of whoever fought off the pack. Perhaps he had heard me coming and fled, worried that I might be another coyote.

"You are safe," I called out. "They are all dead."

There was no answer. I poked around the scrap heaps but found no trace of whoever's scream had brought me here. I couldn't afford to lose more time, so I left the coyotes where they lay and hurried back to where I'd parted from Eirian.

I pushed myself to quick-march through my fatigue, a trick I'd learned as a boy hunting on the plains. I caught up with Eirian and the robot less than a mile away.

"You're injured," Eirian said as I fell into step behind her.

"A wild animal attacked me. A coyote with a corrupted body." I described the scene I'd found and my brief battle. "I could find no sign of whoever the pack attacked, so I returned to you. I thought of butchering the coyotes for rations, but worried their meat might be tainted."

"Wise of you. Here, stop for a moment and I'll heal you."

I stopped as directed and Eirian put one hand on her amulet and the other on my damaged hand. Her eyes took on a faraway look. "Bright Brigh," she intoned, "find the pieces of this man and put them where they belong. Rebuild his form into a perfect whole."

Flickering blue energy lit up Eirian's skin. A circular pattern, like a delicate tattoo, glowed on the left side of her neck. Another appeared above her right eyebrow. Pain surged through my hand as the tears in my flesh wove themselves shut. Eirian's eyelids fluttered. She dropped her hand and her tattoos faded.

"You were glowing," I blurted.

"It is a trait among androids," she replied. She turned from me and strode after the robot.

I hurried after her. "When I fought the coyote, my cuff seemed to activate, granting me exceptional strength. Like when I moved those rocks, but more intense. The cuff glowed just like your tattoos did. With that same blue light."

Eirian's eyes widened. On anyone else, her expression might look mildly interested, but having traveled with her I knew she was registering great shock. "Then perhaps it comes from the same place androids come from."

"Where is that?"

She kept her gaze fixed on the horizon. "I do not know."

Thoughts crowded my mind. If the cuff bore a connection to both the robot and the androids, then perhaps Eirian and I both would find something we sought when the robot reached its destination. We left the rendland haze behind and kept pace with the little machine as it rolled across the plain.

BESTIARY

WE WALKED THROUGH A CANYON THAT SNAKED THROUGH MOUNDS OF DEBRIS PILED SO HIGH THAT IT BLOCKED ALL BUT THE MIDDAY SUN. THE AIR WAS DRY, AND OUR BOOTS KICKED UP REDDISH-BROWN DUST THAT WAS MORE RUST THAN EARTH. I PULLED MY KERCHIEF UP OVER MY NOSE TO AVOID BREATHING THE STUFF. RIGHT AT THAT MOMENT, A METAL CYLINDER BECAME DISLODGED AND TUMBLED DOWN THE FACE OF THE JUNK-HILL. ITS CLATTERING RHYTHM NEARLY MIMICKING A FAMILIAR TUNE. A FIGURE EMERGED FROM THE TOP OF THE MOUND, AND MORE JUNK CASCADED DOWN THE PILE TOWARD US. THE LUMBERING THING MOVED WITH A TWITCHING GAIT AS IT CLAMORED DOWN THE REFUSE. A GORY DRILL WHIRRED ON THE END OF ITS MISSHAPEN ARM, AND ITS METAL JAW CLANKED HUNGRILY BELOW GLOWING EYES. WITH ONE LEAP, THIS METAL-STUDDED CORPSE WAS ON US."

—TSYMULT KRANSIS, SCAVENGER

This volume of the Iron Gods Adventure Path features a bestiary of horrific undead embedded with machinery, strange aliens from the depths of space, robots built for surveillance, and the herald of the clockwork goddess, Brigh.

DEADLY BEASTS AND METAL MENACES

The random encounter table presented here features a number of typical threats the PCs could encounter while exploring Scrapwall. During the course of the adventure, the PCs have a 20% chance of a random encounter every hour they spend exploring Scrapwall, but run across no more than two random encounters per day. Some of these encounters involve creatures from specific encounters in the adventure, so if one of the random encounter rolls results in a specific creature the party has already faced (such as the mutant manticore), roll again.

Since this adventure spans a range of levels, some results might be too simple or too difficult for the PCs, depending on where they are in the course of the adventure. If the result rolled is outside the challenge rating range appropriate for the PCs, roll again or choose a different encounter.

GMs who wish to learn more about Numeria or those looking for other hazards and encounter ideas should check out *Pathfinder Campaign Setting: Numeria, Land of Fallen Stars*. Details on the robot subtype can be found in *Pathfinder Campaign Setting: Inner Sea Bestiary*, and they were reprinted in *Pathfinder Adventure Path #85: Fires of Creation* for convenience.

Dark Scavengers (CR 5): When the *Chrysalis* module fell to Golarion and scattered its cargo across the area, the bulk of it landed on top of a cave that descended into the upper reaches of the Darklands. Millennia later, a clan of dark folk discovered the clogged rift and began collecting the strange materials. The clan studied what they found, and their spellcasters discovered various means to repurpose some of this space junk using methods similar to those employed by the Technic League. A pair of sibling dark slayers (*Pathfinder RPG Bestiary 2 75*) frequently makes trips to the surface to collect more junk to be worked into bizarre contraptions and dangerous weapons. The dark slayers fight anyone who gets between them and their prize.

Night Hunters (CR 7): Not all of the dangers of Scrapwall live in and among the vast field of refuse. A pair of batlike humanoids called sabosans (*Pathfinder RPG Bestiary 3 233*) hunts the area at night, plucking unsuspecting gang members off the streets for an evening meal. The sabosans live in a cave less than a mile from Scrapwall that dives deep below the ground where the two creatures originated. They take to the skies most nights, especially on nights when clouds block the moon's light. The sabosans make use of their echolocation on

SCRAPWALL ENCOUNTERS

d%	Result	Avg. CR	Source
01–04	1d8 acolytes of Hellion	3	See page 36
05–07	1 scrapyard robot	3	See page 43
08–12	1d4 dark creepers	4	*Bestiary* 53
13–16	1 junk golem	4	*Bestiary 4* 132
17–21	1d12 lobotomite	4	See page 24
22–24	1d4 nuglub gremlins	4	*Bestiary 2* 143
25–27	1d4 observer robots	4	See page 88
28–31	1d12 zombies	4	*Bestiary* 288
32–34	Dark Scavengers	5	See below
35–39	1 gearghost	5	*Bestiary 4* 123
40–43	1d8 jinkin gremlins	5	*Bestiary 2* 142
44–48	1d4 rust monsters	5	*Bestiary* 238
49–53	1 spider eater	5	*Bestiary 3* 255
54–57	1d4 dark stalkers	6	*Bestiary* 54
58–60	1d4 giant vultures	6	*Bestiary 3* 284
61–62	1d4 gray oozes	6	*Bestiary* 166
63–66	1 lunarma	6	*Bestiary 4* 185
67–69	1 mutant manticore	6	See page 28
70–74	Rat Infestation	6	See below
75–79	1d8 rust-risen	6	See page 90
80–84	1d12 vexgit gremlins	6	*Bestiary 2* 145
85–87	1 will-o'-wisp	6	*Bestiary* 277
88–90	Night Hunters	7	See below
91–94	1d8 ogres	7	*Bestiary* 220
95–100	Scrapwall Gangs	varies	See below

these dark nights to ambush the people of Scrapwall with their piercing shrieks and disorienting clouds of dust, kicked up by the force of their powerful wings.

Rat Infestation (CR 6): The clutter of Scrapwall allows for countless hiding places for scavengers, and perhaps the most numerous of those residing in Scrapwall are rats. Nestled in a series of tunnels that run through the mounds of trash is a strange tangle of rats that has achieved a heightened consciousness and now rules a pack of rats. This rat king (*Pathfinder RPG Bestiary 4 225*) has the ability to bolster the effectiveness of the disease that rats transmit through their bites. The rat king is guarded by a rat swarm (*Pathfinder RPG Bestiary 232*) and a pair of dire rats (*Bestiary 232*). The rat king has the ability to speak to the dire rats, and it issues commands that aid the creatures in combat.

Scrapwall Gangs (CR varies): Numerous gangs control Scrapwall. If, when rolling for random encounters, this result turns up, the nature of the encounter is related to the area of Scrapwall the PCs are in. For details about gang members with whom the PCs must contend for this encounter, see that particular location in Part 2 of the adventure. If you roll this result while the PCs are in unclaimed territories, reroll this encounter.

LATTEN MECHANISM

This clockwork termite is the size of a rhinoceros and has an oversized head with a humanoid face on it. Multiple apertures along its body sprout tool-wielding limbs, and a human-sized hatch on its abdomen chitters and clicks like a menacing maw.

LATTEN MECHANISM	CR 15

N Large construct (extraplanar, herald[ISG])

Init +8; **Senses** darkvision 60 ft., low-light vision; Perception +22

DEFENSE

AC 31, touch 13, flat-footed 27 (+4 Dex, +18 natural, −1 size)

hp 147 (18d10+48); fast healing 10

Fort +8, **Ref** +12, **Will** +12

DR 10/adamantine and magic; **Immune** acid, construct traits;
  Resist cold 30, fire 30; **SR** 26

OFFENSE

Speed 40 ft., burrow 20 ft., climb 20 ft.

Melee bite +27 (6d8+13 plus grab and 6d8 acid or electricity)

Space 10 ft.; **Reach** 10 ft.

Special Attacks breath weapon (120-ft. line, 12d8 acid or
  electricity damage, Reflex DC 19 half, usable every 1d4
  rounds), constrict (6d8 plus 6d8 acid or electricity), entrap (DC
  19, 1d10 rounds, hardness 8, hp 20), lyre of building

Spell-Like Abilities (CL 18th; concentration +23; save DCs are
  Intelligence-based)
  At will—*dimension door, make whole, move earth, rapid
    repair*[UM]*, soothe construct*[UM]
  3/day—*control construct*[UM]*, fabricate, haste, lightning
    bolt* (DC 18), *major creation, slow* (DC 18), *unbreakable
    construct*[UM]*, wall of iron*

STATISTICS

Str 29, **Dex** 19, **Con** —, **Int** 21, **Wis** 18, **Cha** 16

Base Atk +18; **CMB** +28; **CMD** 42 (50 vs. trip)

Feats Cleave, Combat Expertise, Combat Reflexes, Great
  Fortitude, Gunsmithing[B, UC], Improved Initiative[B], Iron Will[B],
  Lightning Reflexes[B], Power Attack, Stand Still, Toughness,
  Weapon Focus (bite)

Skills Climb +18, Craft (any one) +23, Disable Device +22,
  Knowledge (engineering) +23, Knowledge (religion) +23,
  Perception +22, Sense Motive +13, Spellcraft +22, Use Magic
  Device +12

Languages Abyssal, Celestial, Common, Draconic, Infernal

SQ always armed, change size, create soldiers, double damage
  against objects, emissary, integrated masterwork tools,
  master of crafting

ECOLOGY

Environment any (Axis)

Organization solitary or team (herald plus 1d6 clockwork
  soldiers and 1d6 clockwork servants)

Treasure standard

SPECIAL ABILITIES

Change Size (Su) Latten Mechanism can change its size to
  Huge, Large, or Medium as a standard action, as if using
enlarge person or *reduce person*. This change lasts until it
  changes size again or is killed.

Create Soldiers (Ex) Once per day, Latten Mechanism can
  create up to four clockwork soldiers (*Pathfinder RPG
  Bestiary 3* 57). These soldiers serve it for 1 hour, after which
  they break down into their component parts.

Double Damage Against Objects (Ex) If Latten Mechanism
  makes a full attack against an object or structure, it deals
  double damage.

Integrated Masterwork Tools (Ex) Latten Mechanism
  can extend additional limbs from its body that end in
  masterwork tools suitable for any Craft skill it has ranks in.

Lyre of Building (Su) Latten Mechanism has all of the abilities
  of a *lyre of building* (*Pathfinder RPG Core Rulebook* 522),
  with the same limitations as that item.

Master of Crafting (Ex) Latten Mechanism can spend 10
  minutes reconfiguring itself to allocate its 18 ranks in the
  Craft skill to any specific Craft skills in any combination.
  For example, it can allocate 9 ranks in Craft (armor) and 9
  ranks in Craft (clockwork). All Craft skills are class skills for
  Latten Mechanism.

Latten Mechanism is a defender of constructs and crafters, a living siege engine who prefers the solitude of research and invention to the distractions of battle. Given a massive insectile form to allow it to perform all of its necessary functions, Latten Mechanism's only humanlike feature is the androgynous face built into the top of its insectile head. Able to tear open castle gates, create iron walls, scoop up enemies and crush them in its body, reshape the very earth it stands on, and form complex objects out of raw materials or thin air, Latten Mechanism is a versatile engine of creation and destruction guided by a mechanical conscience that values constructs as much as it does intelligent living creatures.

The herald sees itself as a protective parent of all constructs, especially intelligent ones, and never uses its powers to destroy artificial beings unless it has no other choice; it prefers to neutralize or sideline these opponents until it has the opportunity to reprogram or repurpose them. Much as a true champion of freedom loathes charm spells for temporarily enslaving a person's free will, Latten Mechanism believes spells such as *control construct* are a violation of a sentient construct's free will, and only uses them as a last resort to peacefully end a threat. When confronted by a dangerous construct in an enemy's service, Latten Mechanism has been known to render the construct helpless and flee with it, returning to deal with the construct's master at a later time. The herald is a legend among intelligent constructs, and many come to Brigh's faith after witnessing or experiencing its generosity and leniency.

The herald doesn't speak in battle, as it prefers to fool its opponents into mistaking it for a mindless clockwork foe. Outside of combat, it's curious about its allies' inventions and crafting projects, and it can provide many insights into how the ally might overcome various obstacles to achieve greater successes (although it sometimes needs a few minutes to update its mind with knowledge suitable for the conversation). It can speak equally well out of its termite or humanoid mouth, and sometimes uses both in the same conversation, adding deep emphasis to certain words with its inhuman vocal apparatus. Both voices have a metallic, echoing twang.

The herald's proper name is Latten Mechanism, although it answers to either part of its name individually, or even if its name is used as a title ("the Latten Mechanism"). Its programming allows it to recognize flattery, insults, and threats, although it doesn't really understand the motivations for such things. The easiest way to anger it is to treat it like an unfeeling, unthinking machine or suggest that it could be parceled into useful parts (in the same way that a dragon would object to a casual discussion of how its hide could be made into armor).

ECOLOGY

Latten Mechanism is a created being that has no need to eat or drink. Though it has a need for occasional maintenance to prevent its delicate mechanical parts from seizing up or breaking down, it's effectively immortal. It has no need to reproduce, but it treats all constructs it builds (even the temporary ones) as beloved pets, and is saddened if they are damaged, destroyed, or otherwise compromised. It feels kinship toward mortals who create constructs, so long as those creators are respectful toward their inventions.

The herald has no particular attachment to any mortal race or country, although it has spent more time among humans and the people of Alkenstar than any other kind or place. It holds neither aversion nor affinity to undead creatures—it considers reusing dead body parts to create new entities essentially similar to reusing metal or wood from a destroyed construct to repair or build another.

Because it became self-aware only when Brigh built it out of inanimate parts, it has no fear of death—for it, death is the same as the state of non-consciousness it existed in before its activation. If it was destroyed, but Brigh needed its abilities once more, the goddess would recreate and reawaken it; from the herald's perspective, this wouldn't even be an interruption of its consciousness.

Latten Mechanism has a fondness for small clockwork objects and wind-up toys, such as rolling carts, hopping animals, and music boxes. It collects these treasures much the way noble's child might collect elaborate dolls. A priest who offers such a thing as part of a payment when the herald is called is likely to gain the herald's support, especially if the device features a clever mechanism, such as a dragon toy that utilizes a smokestick to create a miniature breath weapon, or a mechanical spider that utilizes a tanglefoot bag to catch bugs with tiny bursts of sticky webbing.

HABITAT & SOCIETY

The herald spends most of its time on Axis mixing with Brigh's other servitors and pursuing its own research projects. It enjoys the company of axiomites and inevitables, respecting their non-biological anatomies and ever curious about their devotion to law. It sometimes directly intervenes in the mortal world by soothing a rampaging construct that might accidentally kill a genius inventor, but otherwise limits its interactions to those commanded by Brigh.

Among the servitors of Brigh, Latten Mechanism is admired for its crafting skills and devotion to all artificial creatures. Some servitors who become melancholy and long to become true flesh beings seek counsel from the herald, hoping to gain a better appreciation of their mechanical bodies and the uniqueness of their souls.

RHU-CHALIK

Thin tendrils trail from this misshapen sphere. A gray orb hangs beneath the creature like a bulging lidless eye.

RHU-CHALIK	CR 6

XP 2,400

CE Small aberration

Init +7; **Senses** darkvision 60 ft., see in darkness; Perception +10

DEFENSE

AC 18, touch 14, flat-footed 15 (+4 armor, +3 Dex, +1 size)

hp 68 (8d8+32); fast healing 2

Fort +6, **Ref** +5, **Will** +8

Defensive Abilities all-around vision; **Immune** cold, disease

OFFENSE

Speed 5 ft., fly 60 ft. (perfect)

Melee 4 tendrils +10 (1d4+1 plus pain touch)

Special Attacks pain touch, project terror, void transmission

Spell-Like Abilities (CL 10th; concentration +12)

    Constant—*mage armor*

    At will—*detect thoughts* (DC 14), *invisibility, share memory*^{UM} (DC 14)

    1/day—*modify memory* (DC 16)

STATISTICS

Str 12, **Dex** 16, **Con** 19, **Int** 13, **Wis** 14, **Cha** 15

Base Atk +6; **CMB** +6; **CMD** 19

Feats Combat Expertise, Combat Reflexes, Improved Initiative, Weapon Finesse

Skills Bluff +8, Diplomacy +8, Fly +13, Intimidate +10, Perception +10, Sense Motive +7, Stealth +15, Use Magic Device +10

Languages Aklo; telepathy 100 ft.

SQ compression, no breath

ECOLOGY

Environment any

Organization solitary

Treasure none

SPECIAL ABILITIES

Pain Touch (Ex) A rhu-chalik secretes an enzyme that coats its tendrils. When this enzyme comes into contact with a living creature, it causes excruciating pain. Any creature that comes into contact with the enzyme must succeed at a DC 18 Fortitude save or take a –2 penalty on attack rolls, ability checks, and skill checks for 1d4 rounds. If a creature is affected by multiple pain touch attacks, the duration stacks but the penalty doesn't. Creatures that are immune to pain effects are immune to this ability. The save DC is Charisma-based.

Project Terror (Su) As a standard action, a rhu-chalik can harness the fears of any creature it has successfully used *detect thoughts* on within the last minute. This effect creates visions of that creature's most terrible nightmares in the target's mind; the target must succeed at a DC 16 Will save or be frightened and take 1d4 points of Wisdom damage. The save DC is Charisma-based.

Void Transmission (Su) If a creature takes an amount of Wisdom damage from the rhu-chalik's project terror ability that equals or exceeds the creature's Wisdom score, the creature falls unconscious as normal. At that point, the rhu-chalik can take 10 minutes to copy and absorb the creature's entire consciousness and send that consciousness through the void of space to its waiting masters. If the creature's Wisdom damage is healed and the creature is revived prior to the end of this process, this effect fails. If the creature's Wisdom damage is healed after its consciousness is successfully transmitted, the creature awakes disoriented, and takes a –2 penalty on attack rolls, ability checks, and skill checks for 24 hours. This effect otherwise doesn't harm the target, as the target's consciousness isn't eliminated, only duplicated and transmitted.

A rhu-chalik, also called a void wanderer, is an alien entity that scouts for a nebulous collection of space conquerors known as the Dominion of the Black. In addition to ambitions for dominating the universe, they also engage in a curious pursuit: collecting the memories of interesting creatures in the universe into a vast repository of knowledge in hopes of unraveling every secret of existence.

Though they are theoretically capable of traversing the vastness of space to make it to Golarion on their own, the rhu-chaliks encountered here arrived on the crashed spaceship *Divinity*. Years before *Divinity* crashed onto Golarion, the ship's crew discovered rhu-chaliks in a distant galaxy and became intrigued with their unique form. They collected a few specimens and set about observing the enigmatic creatures. Unknown to the scientists, these aliens had allowed their own capture in order to travel to far-flung galaxies where they could explore the thoughts, dreams, and knowledge of thousands upon thousands of races the universe over. The rhu-chaliks kept their strange abilities secret onboard the ship, content to travel in dormancy until the *Divinity* encountered the Dominion of the Black, at which point the creatures shredded the minds of their scientist wardens. Later, as the ship crashed on Golarion, the creatures seeped from the vessel and began their exploration of this new world flush with sentient life.

A rhu-chalik is approximately 3 feet across and weighs only 30 pounds.

ECOLOGY

Rhu-chaliks' anatomy is as alien as their motives. The creatures resemble spongy masses of jet-black tissue, with lidless, pupil-less, grayish-white eyes at their center and four thin tendrils extending from their mass. Rhu-chaliks can hover in atmosphere or float in the dead vacuum of space; they don't need to breathe. They're capable of remaining motionless for decades, and some claim that their life spans may outlast even the stars themselves.

It's assumed that rhu-chaliks are the least powerful of their strange race and exist merely to transmit the minds of interesting creatures they encounter far into the depths of their masters' domain—a starless void beyond the edge of the universe. Those few who have studied rhu-chaliks and survived with their minds intact theorize that these creatures are carefully sculpted to suit their task, and it's likely that their original form has been drastically altered by millennia of specialized breeding into their current dread incarnation. There is no existing information about how these creatures procreate, and it is assumed that they are artificially crafted by their dark masters.

Void wanderers don't feed in the traditional sense, and they lack a mouth or any other orifice that can accept food. Some records retrieved from *Divinity* suggest that the creatures use their tendrils to absorb nutrients through osmosis, but this is incorrect. Rhu-chaliks maintain their bodily form and sustain their lengthy lifespans by feeding off the thoughts and fears of sentient beings. Every emotion has a different flavor to these creatures, and since their feedings are harmless to the sources of their meals, many rhu-chaliks have been observed to dine continuously from the same mind endlessly, prodding different emotions to elicit a new taste as if they were ordering a new course at a banquet.

Habitat & Society

Rhu-chaliks are the lesser cogs of a collective of star-spanning overlords far beyond the powers of Golarion. Rhu-chaliks serve as scouts and traveling collectors that wander through civilizations in search of minds that they can twist with fear and agony. Their ultimate goal is to copy the minds of those they encounter and send the consciousnesses beyond the stars to their masters.

As observers, rhu-chaliks prefer to maintain stealth for as long as possible. These small creatures can compress their spongy bodies into a fraction of their normal size, and then lodge themselves into tight hiding spots so that they can sift through the thoughts of nearby sentient creatures. If discovered, rhu-chaliks leave their hiding places, but they are quick to return once they're confident that they can reestablish secrecy.

Millions of these strange horrors are cast out from their dark domain every moment, hurtling through space until they encounter some alien race or world not yet probed by the dark masters of their native space. From their far-flung redoubt, rhu-chaliks observe the churning cosmos, gathering every speck of information and every thought ever birthed by the minds of a thousand races of alien species.

In the dark space from which they hail, catalogs of entire civilizations hang in a surreal miasma of misplaced minds shrieking out in disembodied agony for all eternity, with their every desire, fear, secret, and scrap of understanding exposed like raw nerves for invasive perusal. The creatures who survive having their consciousnesses copied and transmitted are often unaware of the transmission, and little realize that their most private moments will be pored over endlessly by alien minds.

Rhu-chaliks serve their masters tirelessly, and are as patient as they are long-lived. They rarely make an uncalculated move, and seek only the most prized intellects to cast into the dark beyond for their master's delectations. When exploring distant worlds, rhu-chaliks are not social beings, and they avoid other rhu-chaliks in hopes that their predations won't cause too much overlap in the mind collection clouds of their masters. However, back in their native space, rhu-chaliks number in the billions, and the creatures feed off a countless number of disembodied minds.

ROBOT, OBSERVER

This small robot is reminiscent of a beetle with a pair of pincers extending from the front of its body.

OBSERVER ROBOT	CR 2	

XP 600

N Tiny construct (robot)

Init +2; **Senses** darkvision 60 ft., low-light vision; Perception +15

DEFENSE

AC 18, touch 14, flat-footed 16 (+2 Dex, +4 natural, +2 size)

hp 16 (3d10)

Fort +1, **Ref** +5, **Will** +4

Defensive Abilities all-around vision, hardness 5; **Immune** construct traits

Weaknesses vulnerable to critical hits and electricity

OFFENSE

Speed 20 ft., fly 60 ft. (perfect)

Melee 2 claws +6 (1d2+1), integrated laser torch +6 (1d10)

Ranged integrated stun gun +7 (1d8 plus nonlethal)

Space 2 1/2 ft.; **Reach** 0 ft. (5 ft. with integrated laser torch)

Special Attacks integrated laser torch, integrated stun gun

STATISTICS

Str 12, **Dex** 15, **Con** —, **Int** 10, **Wis** 17, **Cha** 1

Base Atk +3; **CMB** +3; **CMD** 14 (22 vs. trip)

Feats Alertness, Lightning Reflexes

Skills Fly +14, Perception +15, Sense Motive +5, Stealth +11, Survival +5; **Racial Modifiers** +4 Perception

Languages Androffan, Common

SQ camouflage, transmit senses

ECOLOGY

Environment any (Numeria)

Organization solitary or deployment (2–12)

Treasure none

SPECIAL ABILITIES

Camouflage (Ex) An observer robot's outer shell contains color-shifting screens that allow the creature to blend into any background. Though not truly invisible, they are hard to pinpoint. While using this ability, an observer robot gains a +8 racial bonus on Stealth checks and has concealment from creatures more than 5 feet away.

Integrated Laser Torch (Ex) An observer robot is outfitted with an integrated laser torch used to bypass barriers or restraints. When activated, the torch emits a beam of highly focused light, cutting and burning through surfaces up to 6 inches away. Attacks from a laser torch resolve as touch attacks and deal 1d10 points of fire damage. This damage is not modified further by Strength. An observer robot's integrated laser torch is mounted on an extending arm that allows it greater reach. When the laser torch is used as a tool or as a weapon to sunder, its damage bypasses hardness up to 20 points, and damage is not halved (as is normally the case for energy damage applied to objects) unless the object is particularly fire-resistant. A laser torch's cutting beam passes through force fields and force effects without damaging the field. Invisible objects and creatures can't be harmed by a laser torch.

Integrated Stun Gun (Ex) An observer robot has an integrated stun gun built into its head. This weapon uses a sonic amplifier to produce powerful low-frequency blasts of energy that can pummel targets. This weapon has a range increment of 20 feet, and it deals 1d8 points of nonlethal damage. When it scores a critical hit, the robot can attempt a free trip combat maneuver (CMB +13) against the target, which does not provoke attacks of opportunity.

Transmit Senses (Ex) An observer robot is outfitted with a number of sensors, cameras, and microphones that allow it to record events and transmit them to another location. An observer robot can record up to 12 hours of audio and video. An observer robot's communications can be keyed to a commset^TG or other similar device, and it can broadcast everything it can see or hear to this device as long as it is within 1 mile. The signal strength can be enhanced with a signal booster^TG. An observer robot can also transmit its senses to another observer robot. A signal has difficulty penetrating solid barriers. A signal is blocked by 1 foot of metal, 5 feet of stone, or 20 feet of organic matter. Force fields do not block signals. Broadcasting functions like a *scrying* sensor, allowing the viewer to hear and see what the observer robot is experiencing. The viewer gains the benefits of any nonmagical special abilities the observer robot has tied to its senses (such as low-light vision), but the viewer uses her own Perception skill. This ability doesn't allow magically or supernaturally enhanced senses to work through it, even if both the observer robot and the viewer possess them.

Designed for reconnaissance, observer robots are deployed to serve as the eyes and ears of their controllers. Because they're intelligent and able to make their own decisions, observer robots are suited for exploring without supervision, recording their observations so that they can relay the images and sounds to their creators. The outer hull of an observer robot and its wings are covered in a network of tiny screens that can display images of the robots' surroundings, which grants the observer robot a form of camouflage that allows it to clandestinely observe its subjects.

The statistics above represent the most common observer robots, but some models have enhanced senses that allow them to see in darkness or see invisible creatures. Some even have olfactory sensors that effectively smell their environment and test the surrounding air for impurities that would harm their creators. Observer robots deployed in hostile environments might be outfitted with more formidable weaponry than the standard stun gun and laser torch.

An observer robot is approximately 20 inches long and weighs 8 pounds.

OBSERVER ROBOT SWARM — CR 10

XP 9,600

N Tiny construct (robot, swarm)

Init +8; **Senses** darkvision 60 ft., low-light vision; Perception +30

DEFENSE

AC 23, touch 17, flat-footed 18 (+4 Dex, +1 dodge, +6 natural, +2 size)

hp 117 (18d10+18)

Fort +6, **Ref** +12, **Will** +12

Defensive Abilities all-around vision, hardness 10, swarm traits; **Immune** construct traits

Weaknesses vulnerable to electricity

OFFENSE

Speed 30 ft., fly 60 ft. (perfect)

Melee swarm (4d6 plus distraction and 2d6 fire)

Space 10 ft.; **Reach** 0 ft.

Special Attacks distraction (DC 19)

STATISTICS

Str 12, **Dex** 19, **Con** —, **Int** 11, **Wis** 18, **Cha** 3

Base Atk +18; **CMB** —; **CMD** —

Feats Alertness, Dodge, Following Step Improved Initiative, Improved Lightning Reflexes, Iron Will, Lightning Reflexes, Step Up, Toughness

Skills Fly +20, Perception +30, Sense Motive +10, Stealth +20, Survival +9; **Racial Modifiers** +4 Perception

Languages Androffan, Common

SQ camouflage, transmit senses

ECOLOGY

Environment any (Numeria)

Organization solitary or cloud (2–5)

Treasure none

SPECIAL ABILITIES

Camouflage (Ex) An observer robot's outer shell contains color-shifting screens that allow the creature to blend into the background. Though not truly invisible, they are hard to pinpoint. While using this ability, an observer robot gains a +8 racial bonus on Stealth checks and has concealment from creatures more than 5 feet away.

Transmit Senses (Ex) Though observer robot swarms still maintain the ability to transmit their senses to a receiver like a normal observer robot, these rogue robots rarely do so.

Observer robots were sometimes deployed in groups that were dependent on each other. Their instruments were networked to form a web of sensors spread out over a wide area to retrieve superior surveillance for their masters. Years after these networked robots ceased receiving orders, numerous observer robots rewrote their programming and assembled into collectives that numbered up to 1,000 individual observer robots. These swarms emerge from buried wreckage in dangerous metallic clouds that scour, confound, and burn creatures they attack.

While swarms are typically chaotic, roiling clouds of creatures, observer robot swarms are highly organized, with hundreds of the tiny robots moving in synchronized patterns as they fly through the air. When observer robot swarms attack, the screens on their outer hulls flicker with disorienting colors that leave their enemies nauseated. They can also organize themselves into a matrix to display composite images across the screens on their collective shells. Treating their individual screens like pixels, observer robot swarms can form moving images of things that they have recorded such as displaying the terror-stricken face of their last victim. These robot swarms even cleverly use this technique to disguise themselves as churning clouds, flickering fires, or even other swarms such as bats or wasps.

Since observer robot swarms spend much of their processing power transmitting and sharing senses with other robots in the swarm, they rarely transmit to other devices. Their recordings are shared among the collective, making harvesting recorded data from them extremely difficult.

RUST-RISEN

Miscellaneous bits of rusted machinery are fused to the body of this shambling corpse.

RUST-RISEN	CR 2

XP 600

CE Medium undead

Init +5; **Senses** darkvision 60 ft.; Perception +7

DEFENSE

AC 15, touch 11, flat-footed 14 (+1 Dex, +4 natural)

hp 19 (3d8+6)

Fort +3, **Ref** +2, **Will** +4

Defensive Abilities absorb electricity; **Immune** undead traits

Weaknesses malfunction

OFFENSE

Speed 30 ft.

Melee arm drill +5 (1d6+3), metal jaw +5 (1d6+3)

STATISTICS

Str 17, **Dex** 13, **Con** —, **Int** 5, **Wis** 12, **Cha** 14

Base Atk +2; **CMB** +5; **CMD** 16

Feats Improved Initiative, Power Attack

Skills Intimidate +6, Perception +7, Stealth +5; **Racial Modifiers** +2 Perception

Languages Common

SQ augmentations

ECOLOGY

Environment any

Organization solitary, pair, or pack (3–12)

Treasure none

SPECIAL ABILITIES

Absorb Electricity (Ex) When a rust-risen is damaged by electricity, it takes no damage (as if immune). Instead, the rust-risen gains 1 temporary hit point for every 4 points of damage it would have taken. A rust-risen can only have a number of temporary hit points equal to 150% of its hit point total. These temporary hit points disappear 1 hour later. If a rust-risen takes more than double its normal hit point total in electricity damage from a single attack, the creature is destroyed.

Augmentations (Ex) Rust-risen have various pieces of malfunctioning machinery embedded in their bodies. Each of these augmentations provides the rust-risen with different abilities. A rust-risen has one augmentation plus one additional augmentation for every 3 Hit Dice the creature possesses (typically 2 for most rust-risen). The rust-risen presented here has the arm drill and metal jaw augmentations. See the next page for other augmentations.

Malfunction (Ex) The machinery embedded in a rust-risen functions unpredictably in stressful situations. When a rust-risen enters combat, there is a cumulative 1% chance each round that it malfunctions. This chance resets to 0% 1 minute after combat ends. When a rust-risen malfunctions, it takes a –2 penalty on attack rolls, saving throws, skill checks, and ability checks for 1d4 minutes.

Rust-risen lurk n the burned-out husks of ancient space-faring vessels and among the grease and blood stained laboratories of mad, technologist necromancers. These hideous undead mockeries riddled with the remnants of ancient technology—rotting creatures, outfitted with twitching relics of a space-faring race, that prey on the living by tearing their victims to shreds with gnashing drills, vivisecting scalpels, and flailing exsanguination tubes.

ECOLOGY

Necromancers with a twisted affinity for technology often forgo the usual ghoul or zombie minions for a rust-risen ally. Far from mindless, rust-risen possess limited memories of their lives before undeath, though these recollections are more like misshapen shadows flickering on the walls of their minds, and are often distorted and highly inaccurate.

Habitat & Society

Rust-risen possess the unnatural hunger for the living shared by other undead, but they also maintain a strange obsession with technological artifacts. It's not uncommon when breaching a rust-risen lair to find it filled with baubles, gizmos, and other technological oddities—even schematics which rust-risen cannot make sense of. Rust-risen collect such items, which appear to give them some semblance of comfort in their rotting horror of an existence. Rust-risen also seek sources of electrical power, finding them comforting in the same way a warm bath soothes living flesh. If denied access to an electrical power source, rust-risen become sluggish and despondent, but spring to activity as soon as they are exposed to electricity.

Rust-risen are always bonded to their creator, serving them as loyally as an animal companion does its master. They rely on their creator to keep their malfunctioning technology from completely breaking down. Over time however, their bond grows into obsession; eventually it becomes an uncontrollable desire for their master to join them in undeath. Such obsessed rust-risen often overpower their necromancer overlords, who awaken to find themselves on an operating table, their machine-studded monstrosities hovering busily over their extracted viscera.

If a rust-risen's creator is destroyed, the undead becomes despondent and lost. It wanders, avoiding civilization and hovering at the fringes of communities, preying on stragglers and wallowing in misanthropic misery. At the same time, it constantly seeks the aid of anyone who can keep it from breaking down. This duality means that the mood of an uncontrolled rust-risen is nigh-impossible to predict.

Rust-Risen Augmentations

As rust-risen are cobbled together from dead bodies augmented with barely-functioning machinery, no two are exactly alike. Some technologically minded necromancers with enough raw materials and a consistent design plan try to make their rust-risen conform to a template, but most packs of rust-risen are motley and violent amalgamations of flesh and steel.

A GM can further modify rust-risen in their games with augmentations of their own creation, but they should be no more powerful than those described below.

Additional Appendage: Some rust-risen are augmented with an additional mechanical limb. A rust-risen with this augmentation gains a slam attack that deals damage appropriate for its size (1d4 for most rust-risen). This arm can manipulate objects as well as a normal arm, but cannot be used to wield a weapon.

Antifreeze: A rust-risen with this augmentation has an embedded series of tubes connected to a pump that keeps a chemical flowing through its body, preventing ice from forming inside it. The rust-risen gains resistance 5 to cold.

Arm Drill: A rust-risen with this augmentation has a deadly, spinning drill grafted onto its forearm. The rust-risen can use the drill to make a melee attack that deals 1d6 points of bludgeoning, piercing, and slashing damage.

Cling Hooks: A rust-risen with this augmentation has barbed hooks grafted into its arms and legs. The rust-risen gains a +4 racial bonus on Climb checks and a +4 racial bonus on combat maneuvers to grapple opponents.

Cutting Arm: A rust-risen with this augmentation has one of its forearms replaced with a functional laser torch. The rust-risen deals 1d10 points of fire damage as a touch attack. This damage is not modified further by Strength. When the laser torch is used as a tool or as a weapon to sunder, damage dealt by it bypasses hardness up to 20 points and isn't halved (as is normally the case for energy damage applied to objects) unless the object is fire resistant. A laser torch's cutting beam passes through a force field and force effect without damaging that field. Invisible objects and creatures cannot be harmed by a laser torch.

Eviscerator: A rust-risen with the eviscerator augmentation has a number of twisting blades, reciprocating saws, and spinning drills built into its chest. The rust-risen deals an additional 1d8 points of damage when grappling.

Exsanguination Tubes: A rust-risen with exsanguination tubes can drain blood from creatures it has grappled. If the rust-risen establishes or maintains a pin, it bleeds the target, dealing 1 point of Constitution damage.

Metal Jaw: A rust-risen with this augmentation has a metal jaw replacing its natural one. The rust-risen gains a bite attack that deals damage appropriate for its size (1d6 points of damage for most rust-risen).

Multi-tool: A rust-risen with this augmentation has at least one of its hands replaced with a variety of tools. The rust-risen gains a +4 competence bonus on Disable Device checks and is considered to be trained in that skill. The rust-risen also gains a +2 competence bonus on one specific Craft skill.

Steel Clad: A rust-risen with this augmentation has sheets of metal riveted to is body. The rust-risen gains a +2 natural armor bonus.

Tripod: A rust-risen with this augmentation has an additional mechanical leg. The rust-risen gains a +2 bonus to CMD against overrun and trip attempts and a +2 bonus on Acrobatics when moving on narrow surfaces or uneven ground. The rust-risen isn't considered flat-footed nor does it lose its Dexterity bonus to AC when using Acrobatics in this way.

The Choking Tower

By Ron Lundeen

The Lords of Rust and their strange god have been defeated, but in doing so, Numeria's newest heroes have uncovered a greater threat than the one posed by the gang of bandits and its mad god. An even more powerful deity is rising in the enigmatic Silver Mount, but before the heroes can confront it, they must uncover the legacy of this strange deity's first worshiper. Clues point to the technophobic town of Iadenveigh—a farming community with its own need for heroes. What role could the mysterious Smoke Wizard of the Choking Tower play in this unfolding threat? Will the heroes be ready for their inevitable battle with Numeria's Iron God?

Iadenveigh Gazetteer

By Ron Lundeen

Built on and around a hill near the Dagger River, Iadenveigh is an oasis of civilization in the wastes of Numeria. But visitors should beware, as Iadenveigh has outlawed the technological wonders found throughout the region.

Missions in the Wastelands

By Patrick Renie

Discover more of the wonders to be found in the land of super-science! Use these three exciting encounters—complete with tactical maps of the locations—to expand your Iron Gods Adventure Path experience.

And More!

The journey continues through the wastes of Numeria in the Pathfinder's Journal, by Amber E. Scott, plus five new monsters in the Pathfinder Bestiary.

Subscribe to Pathfinder Adventure Path

The Iron Gods Adventure Path continues! Don't miss out on a single exciting volume—visit **paizo.com/pathfinder** and subscribe today to have each Pathfinder Adventure Path, Pathfinder Campaign Setting, Pathfinder Player Companion, Pathfinder Module, Pathfinder Tales, and Pathfinder Accessories product delivered to your door! Also, be sure to check out the free *Iron Gods Player's Guide*, available now!

Explore New Horizons

Pathfinder Tales

Amazing Stories Set in the Pathfinder Campaign Setting

ISBN-13: 978-1-60125-618-8 Paperback $9.99

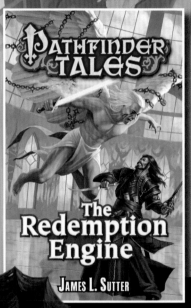

Pathfinder Tales
The Redemption Engine
James L. Sutter

When murdered sinners fail to show up in Hell, it's up to Salim Ghadafar, an atheist warrior forced to solve problems for the goddess of death, to track down the missing souls. In order to do so, Salim will need to descend into the anarchic city of Kaer Maga, following a trail that ranges from Hell's iron cities to the gates of Heaven itself. Along the way, he'll be aided by a host of otherworldly creatures, a streetwise teenager, and two warriors of the mysterious Iridian Fold. But when the missing souls are the scum of the earth, and the victims devils themselves, can anyone really be trusted?

From acclaimed author James L. Sutter comes a sequel to *Death's Heretic*, ranked #3 on Barnes & Noble's Best Fantasy Releases of 2011!

When the aristocratic Vishov family is banished from their native Ustalav due to underhanded politics, they're faced with a choice: fade slowly into obscurity, or strike out for the nearby River Kingdoms and establish a new holding on the untamed frontier. For Lady Tyressa Vishov, the decision is simple. Together with her children and loyal retainers, she'll forge a new life in the infamous Echo Wood, and neither bloodthirsty monsters nor local despots will stop her from reclaiming her family honor. Yet the shadow of Ustalavic politics is long, and even in a remote and lawless territory, there may be those determined to see the Vishov family fail...

From *New York Times* best-selling author Michael A. Stackpole comes a new novel of frontier adventure set in the world of the Pathfinder Roleplaying Game and the new Pathfinder Online massively multiplayer online roleplaying game.

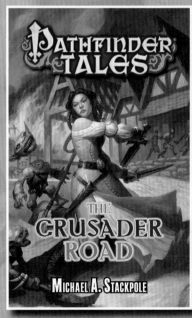

Pathfinder Tales
The Crusader Road
Michael A. Stackpole

ISBN-13: 978-1-60125-657-7 Paperback $9.99

paizo.com